The Scopes Trial

The SCOPES TRIAL

The State of Tennessee v. John Thomas Scopes

by Mary Lee Settle

Illustrated with photographs

FRANKLIN WATTS, INC.   845 Third Avenue · New York, N.Y. 10022

SBN 531-02027-4
Library of Congress Catalog Card Number: 73-181449
© Copyright 1972 by Mary Lee Settle
Printed in the United States of America

Contents

1

Darwin and the Beagle

On December 27, 1831, Charles Darwin, a newly graduated English divinity student, went aboard H.M.S. *Beagle,* a ten-gun brig commanded by Captain Robert Fitz Roy of the Royal Navy. Young Darwin had signed on as an unpaid naturalist for a five-year voyage around the world.

Darwin was twenty-two years old at the time. His qualifications for the job of naturalist were those of a student and an amateur. He had studied under Adam Sedgwick and J. S. Henslow, the two men with the most interesting scientific minds of that time at Cambridge University. This studying was outside Darwin's regular work to prepare himself for the ministry. He already was what his uncle Josiah Wedgwood called "a man of enlarged curiosity," though he had had very little real experience as a naturalist. A taxidermist in Edinburgh had taught him to stuff animals, and he had gone on a geological tour of Wales.

More important than all this, Darwin had begun, as he would for the rest of his life, to put the questions of a child through the mind of a genius—such questions as "What teaches the woodpecker to walk up a tree?"

It was this quality of curiosity that led Henslow, his teacher of botany and also a minister, to recommend Darwin for the voyage. Henslow had received a letter from Captain Fitz Roy, who offered to give up part of his own cabin to any young man who would volunteer to go with him without pay as a naturalist.

The *Beagle* was one of two ships bound on a scientific mission—to survey the seas for the British Admiralty. When British ships of that time went on such voyages, they often carried men of other sciences with them. Besides, Captain Fitz Roy wanted someone to keep him company during the long sailing. As the captain aboard a nineteenth-century British man-of-war, he held one of the loneliest positions on earth.

At that point, Darwin did not question his religious beliefs. As he said in his *Autobiography,* "I did not then in the least doubt the strict and literal truth of every word of the Bible."

The *Beagle* set sail from Devil's Point, Devonport. Darwin had never before been out of Europe. As the ship sailed south through the stormy Bay of Biscay and then into the calmer waters of the South Atlantic a new world of delight opened up for him. He saw for the first time tropical islands, pure white sands, dense rain forests. Faced with so much beauty, the young man had to remind himself from time to time why he had come. In Brazil, he wrote:

> The day has passed delightfully. Delight itself, however, is a weak term to express the feelings of a naturalist who, for the first time, has wandered by himself in a Brazilian forest. The elegance of the grasses, the novelty of the parasitical plants, the beauty of the flowers, the glossy green of the foliage, but above all the general luxuriance of the vegetation, filled me with admiration. A most paradoxical mixture

of sound and silence pervades the shady parts of the wood. The noise from the insects is so loud that it may be heard even in a vessel anchored several hundred yards from the shore; yet within the recesses of the forest a universal silence appears to reign. To a person fond of natural history, such a day as this brings with it a deeper pleasure than he can ever hope to experience again.

For three years Darwin traveled on the *Beagle,* often living ashore for weeks at a time, observing, cataloging, collecting the various animals and plants he saw, always curious, always observant. Then, in September, 1835, he sighted the Galapagos Islands, a group of fifteen large islands and many smaller ones lying under the Equator in the Pacific Ocean near Ecuador. Herman Melville described them this way:

It is to be doubted whether any spot of earth can, in desolateness, furnish a parallel to this group. Abandoned cemeteries of long ago, old cities by piecemeal tumbling to their ruin, these are melancholy enough; but, like all else which has but once been associated with humanity, they still awaken in us some thought of sympathy, however sad. . . . But the special curse . . . is, that to them change never comes; neither the change of seasons nor of sorrows. . . . While already reduced to the lees of fire, ruin itself can work little more upon them.

Melville saw an ancient, unchanging world, but to the young scientist Darwin the Galapagos were a new world. He wrote of the islands:

Considering the small size of these islands, we feel the more astonished at the number of their aboriginal beings, and at their confined range. Seeing every height crowned with its crater, and the boundaries of most of the lava streams still distinct, we are led to believe that within a period geologically recent the unbroken ocean was here spread out. Hence, both in space and time, we seem to be brought somewhere near to that great fact—that mystery of mysteries —the first appearance of new beings on this earth.

Darwin found himself surrounded by "new birds, new reptiles, new shells, new insects, new plants." It was not all work for the excited young scientist; there was play as well, sometimes with the giant turtles.

I was always amused when overtaking one of these great monsters, as it was quietly pacing along, to see how suddenly, the instant I passed, it would draw in its head and legs, and uttering a deep hiss fall to the ground with a heavy sound, as if struck dead. I frequently got on their backs, and then giving a few raps on the hinder part of their shells, they would rise up and walk away;—but I found it very difficult to keep my balance.

For the most part, these strange and isolated islands had been inhabited since their beginning only by animals other than man: strange reptiles, lizards up to fifteen inches long, the great tortoises, and birds. Darwin spent just over four weeks going from island to island of the Galapagos, but those four weeks were to be decisive ones not only for Darwin but also for the future of man's thinking about himself and his place in the world.

On the Galapagos, Darwin noticed finches that were modified according to the needs of survival on the particular island they inhabited. On one island, where the birds' food was insects, they had small beaks. On another, where the finches lived on seeds they had to break open, their beaks were larger and more powerful. At the time, Darwin only asked himself questions, as he always had, about what he had noticed. He wrote in his journal:

> When I see these islands in sight of each other and possessed of but a scanty stock of animals, tenanted by these birds but slightly different in structure and filling the same place in nature, I must suspect they are only varieties. . . . If there is the slightest foundation for these remarks, the zoology of archipelagoes will be well worth examining, for such facts would undermine the stability of species.

In 1839, Darwin published a book written from his journals of the voyage. He called his book *The Voyage of the Beagle*. It was half an adventure story and half a fascinating new view of the natural world. In it he again went over the problem of the strange islands, of why the living things had changed and become modified.

> It is the circumstance that several of the islands possess their own species of the tortoise, mocking thrush, finches, and numerous plants, these species having the same general habits, occupying analogous situations, and obviously filling the same place in the natural economy of this archipelago, that strikes me with wonder.

What aroused his wonder was that while most of the islands were within sight of one another, the species had not interbred and modified each other. Soil, climate, and land height were all much the same, but he pointed out that very strong currents of the sea ran between the islands. He noted an almost complete freedom from gales, and wrote of the profound depths of the sea around the Galapagos. The most important peculiarity of all to him, though, was the islands' recent volcanic origin—that

newness, that incredible newness—for Darwin was already
thinking in terms of millions of years. "One is astonished at the
amount of creative force," he wrote.

It was as if he had stumbled on the miracle of a part of the
world slowly being born.

All thoughts of becoming a clergyman in the church had
long since been forgotten. The young man who asked so many
questions was ready to take a place at the forefront of British
natural science. For twenty years he went over and over the
problem of the islands and the differences in their little finches.
A new theory of how animals evolved into different species was
forming in his mind.

Finally, in 1859, he published what he called his "little
work" on the theory of the evolution of species by what he believed was "natural selection." He called his book *The Origin
of Species*.

The theories in the book touched questions in men's minds
that had been stirring and fermenting to the point where mental revolution seemed only to need an event to set it off. It is
difficult now to imagine the force with which the publication of
Darwin's theory split the public mind. Not only the scientific
but the religious community was sundered, first in England,
then in the rest of the world.

The *Times* of London sent the book to Thomas Henry Huxley, the most brilliant zoologist in England, to review. When he
read it, he said, "How extremely stupid not to have thought of
that," and proceeded to appoint himself, as he said, Darwin's
bulldog in the fight that followed.

What was the fight about? No less than this: for two thousand years Western man had been taught in his churches, had
held as immutable dogma, and had burned his fellow creatures
for questioning, that God had constructed the world in six days
and had made the first man in his own image and had called
him Adam.

Darwin posed instead the idea that man had descended, through millions of years of gradual change, from less complicated life forms, probably from the single-celled protozoa. In Darwin's view, man had won his place on earth, and even his erect form and his conscious brain, through selective survival. In other words, man "worked" better in his environment than many animals, such as the great lizards, which had become extinct. Darwin conceived of all the animals with adaptable hands and feet, the primates, as descended from a common ancestor, but modified, as the Galapagos finches had been, into separate species. In these species he included man, the apes, and the monkeys.

Was the creation of man a piercing revelation or the result of long eons of natural evolution from a lower order of animals? Was man descended from among the angels, or risen from among the animals? To those men who first heard Darwin's theory there seemed to be no compromise. Scientists, led by Huxley, and theologians, led by Bishop Wilberforce, demanded a choice between Darwin and the Book of Genesis.

The debate was to be long and heartbreaking. It would not near its end until a hot afternoon in a small American town sixty-six years later. There was never, of course, to be a clear-cut right side and wrong side, but only a tragic clash of dogma, poetry, theory, and fact. Edmund Gosse, as a little boy, saw his father, the English naturalist Philip Gosse, go through this mental torture. Besides being a scientist, Philip Gosse had been converted to one of the most extreme of English Puritan sects —the Plymouth Brethren. Years later, Edmund Gosse wrote:

Through my father's brain . . . there rushed two kinds of thought, each absorbing, each convincing, yet totally irreconcilable. There is a peculiar agony in the paradox that truth has two forms, each of them indisputable, yet each antagonistic to the other. It was this discovery, that there were two theories of physical life, each of which was true, but the truth of each incompatible with the truth of the other, which shook the spirit of my father with perturbation. It was not, really, a paradox, it was a fallacy, if he could only have known it, but he allowed the turbid volume of superstition to drown the delicate stream of reason. He took one step in the service of truth, and then he drew back in an agony, and accepted the servitude of error.

Gosse's tragic dilemma was repeated all over England among thinking and religious men.

2

Revelation or Revolution?

In 1860, Abraham Lincoln was elected President of the United States. A great war was about to be waged between the Northern and Southern states of a splintered Union. Such a holocaust tended to hold back and obscure scientific questioning. It tended also to do something worse to the American mind. Because of the passions of the war and of the shaky, prejudiced peace that followed it, men did not so much digest or question; instead, they used as tools any theories or ideas that would strengthen argument rather than change or open minds.

The Darwinian theory was no exception. Misquoted and misunderstood, it became a term of abuse between liberals and conservatives, between atheists and men of God, and after the war, between the progressive, forward-thinking North and the conservative, defensive South.

To many, it shed some light at least on the appalling and senseless events of the war. Charles Loring Brace, a leading reformer, read this into it:

. . . if the Darwinian theory be true, the law of natural
selection applies to all the moral history of mankind, as well
as the physical. Evil must die ultimately as the weaker element, in the struggle with good.

It was not a long step from there to thinking of the impov-
erished, defeated South as somehow "lower" on the scale of social evolution than the up-and-coming, triumphant North.

By the 1870's the idea of natural selection dominated
American natural science in the northern universities. Science
was forward-looking. The humanities were "old-fogeyism." The
question of evolution spread down to the student bodies, and
colleges buzzed with controversy and discussion. The clergy
raged. Teachers were fired from universities. But Darwinism,
as it was being called, steadily gained ground.

In his book *Christianity and Positivism,* the Reverend
James McCosh, president of Princeton University, accepted the
theory as not being against the teachings of the church. When
Henry Ward Beecher, the most popular American preacher of
his time, was won over to that point of view, the most important pulpit in the country fell to the evolutionists. Already the
followers of Darwin were beginning to sound more like a political party than a school of scientific thought.

While the theologians argued, a more powerful and in
many ways far more sinister part of the American public was
taking up Darwinism and combining it with the ideas of Herbert Spencer, the English social philosopher. Spencer saw Darwin's theory as a biological rule that could be applied socially
and economically to his own theory of the survival of the fittest.

Nothing suited the conscience of the Gilded Age after the
Civil War more than the idea of the survival of the fittest. This
was the Age of Progress, and any weakness, any poverty, any
frailty that stood in the way of progress had to be swept aside
almost as a religious necessity. Progress was actually called

"not an accident, but a necessity."

The new postwar American was a go-getter without any unpatriotic questioning of where he was going and what he was getting, and Herbert Spencer was his prophet, quoted in arguments around the pot-bellied stoves and on the cracker barrels all over the country. No one defined better than he did the economic and political "individualism" that was leading the country on a fantastic spree of progress. More Americans swore by Spencer than any other philosopher. His ultraconservative books sold like best-selling novels.

The poor, he wrote in *Social Statics*, one of his most popular works, should be eliminated, "to clear the world of them, and make room for better." In an even more brutal vein, Spencer carried his conclusions about the poor to their logical end. "If they are sufficiently complete to live, they DO live, and it is well they should live. If they are not sufficiently complete to live, they die, and it is best they should die."

America's freely competitive industrial capitalism was off to a galloping postwar boom, and its Golden Rule had been spoken by Herbert Spencer. Evolutionary theory had become a battle cry of the new radical free enterprise. Its thinking could not be called conservative, since conservative social ideas had had at least a sense of social responsibility. The followers of Spencer had none. They used his saying as an excuse for the most brutal and irresponsible antisocial economic philosophy ever followed in America.

Reformers began to be worried about the outcome. Terms like "vested interests," "monopolies," "trusts" began to litter political talk.

William Jennings Bryan, the leader of radical reform in America, read Darwin's later book, *The Descent of Man,* and said that such teaching would "weaken the cause of democracy and strengthen class pride and the power of wealth."

Darwin's theory had gone an almost unrecognizable way from the Galapagos Islands and the little finches.

3 ✍

The Knight in Shining Armor

The first victims of the buoyant, "devil-take-the-hindmost" business methods were, of course, the workingmen and the new immigrant labor force that was being brought over by entire villages from Scotland, from Italy, and from Ireland. Wherever there was poverty to exploit, such captains of industry as Henry Frick and Andrew Carnegie transported immigrants by the thousands as cheap labor for the mines, for the factories, and often to break the strikes of the native workingmen who were beginning to try to defend themselves by forming unions. The native American who went down from his hill farm to work at the coal face or in the iron mines, when mining started all along the Allegheny chain of mountains, felt the threat of cheap immigrant labor; he began to connect the word "foreigner" with the exploitation of big business.

The second group of victims were the midwestern farmers. Once they had been self-sustaining, courted and flattered by the politicians from Jackson on into thinking they were "the backbone of America." Sturdy, with a stern religious sense, they had shown a spirit and an independence in daily life unmatched anywhere else in the country. They were yeomen of honor—until the railroads came.

Then, almost without realizing it, the farmers, seduced by credit, new machinery, and store-bought clothes from the cities, turned into small businessmen with one crop that they had to sell in order to buy necessities. Where once the farmer had provided most of the food and clothing for himself and his family, now he was dependent on the railroads to ship his goods, on city markets, and on wholesalers who paid little and sold dear. Worst of all, he suffered from something he could neither control nor understand—big-business manipulation of stocks and currency. He had no understanding of gold standards and international finance; he only knew that the dollar he owed the bank had suddenly inflated to three times what its value had been when he borrowed so easily to buy new machinery. What had once cost a bushel of wheat now cost three. The prices of his crops were controlled by city men he could not see and powers he could only resent.

He was left with crops he could not afford to ship to market. "Many a time," the historian Vernon L. Parrington remembered, "have I warmed myself by the kitchen stove in which ears of corn were burning briskly, popping and crackling in the jolliest fashion. And if while we sat around such a fire, watching the year's crop go up the chimney, the talk sometimes became bitter . . . who will wonder?"

Then, as if they had constructed him, the victims found a perfect leader. He had been born into their kind of world—in Illinois. He shared their Puritan code. He had even been saved for Jesus at a revival meeting. He had been educated at a small midwestern college. He stood for everything they stood for—home and church and country. He respected and loved his parents and he did not question or ridicule the fundamental virtues taught by them.

William Jennings Bryan burst upon the American political scene at the Democratic convention of 1896. It was there that, with his flowing hair and his handsome strong face, he stood up, the most brilliant evangelical orator the country had ever heard, and called out, in a good, loud, beautiful voice, the speech that made him famous and gave him the Democratic nomination for the presidency of the United States.

Having behind us the producing masses of this nation and the world, supported by the commercial interests, the laboring interests, and the toilers everywhere, we will answer their demand for a gold standard by saying to them: You shall not press down upon the brow of labor this crown of thorns; you shall not crucify mankind upon a cross of gold.

The people he defended so eloquently loved him as they did their preachers or their matinee idols. He was a little of both, but at the same time, he was, in President Wilson's words, "an utterly sincere man." But the President added, "That is what makes him dangerous."

Bryan was defeated three times for the presidency. He polled large numbers of popular votes, but his opponents always polled enough more, and in the right states, to win. Bryan had the strange quality of being strengthened by defeat. He even made fun of it. "The Bible says that two shall put ten thousand to flight," he said. "I am looking for the other man!" The people loved him even more in defeat than they had in victory. The East vilified him as, in the new dawn of progress, it vilified the rest of America, leaving deep and almost ineradicable scars of resentment and distrust.

For thirty stormy years in American national politics, Bryan, the Peerless Leader, the Knight in Shining Armor, the Great Commoner, not only considered, but listened to, represented, and mirrored the hopes and indeed the mentality of the

William Jennings Bryan in 1896. His "Cross of Gold" speech at the Democratic National Convention in that year won him the party's presidential nomination, though he was only thirty-six years old.
(PHOTO FROM CHARLES PHELPS CUSHING)

common American people. He was the perfect radical reformer in the Age of Progress. He had fought for the farmers, for peace, for woman suffrage, for an income tax, for government ownership of public utilities, and for free silver. He believed in America and in God, in progress, and in the absolute infallibility of the people's choice, and he never ceased or faltered in those beliefs. He spoke his creed over and over again:

> I assert that the people of the United States . . . have sufficient patriotism and sufficient intelligence to sit in judgment on every question which has arisen or which will arise no matter how long our government will endure. The great political questions are in their final analysis great moral questions.

All through his career as America's most powerful orator, Bryan connected politics with religion in the unquestioning revivalist tradition of his Illinois youth, that of the Bible and the voice of God. He demanded of religion that it guide him and his followers through a new age of scientific discovery and through the new techniques of business manipulation that were making the common people the victims. Somehow, for Bryan's followers, the people of the vast backcountry of America, the two things—the mind and money—became connected, and dangerous.

The incapacity of these people to understand a new and threatening world made them bitter and resentful. A darker, more sinister, note crept into their beliefs. The farmer, who had once based his politics on something he could understand—a freer currency to help him pay his debt to the bank—now had a new enemy, the mind that excluded him from understanding and derided his ignorance.

As the years went on, Bryan spoke out more and more for the backcountry people. Not facts or time or circumstances changed him. His special quality of innocent greatness showed itself in a last gesture as he resigned as secretary of state in Woodrow Wilson's cabinet. When Bryan's repeated protests to President Wilson against actions that he knew were leading the country into World War I were ignored, he gave up the only national office he had ever held.

"The issue involved," he said in a note of resignation to President Wilson on June 8, 1915, "is of such moment that to remain a member of the cabinet would be as unfair to you as it would be to the cause which is nearest to my heart, namely, the prevention of war."

Bryan knew that his place in American national politics was lost by the move, but it did not alter his decision. "I think this will destroy me," he told another member of the cabinet, "but whether it does or not I must do my duty according to my conscience."

Later, he sadly took leave of the rest of the cabinet. "I go out into the dark," he said, and added, "but I have many friends who would die for me."

He was right. He lost his power as a leader of the Democratic party—partly, it was said, because of the invention of the loudspeaker. Once his voice had been the only one strong enough to reach all the delegates. Now a whisper could be heard through the new machines. Men of less lung power and more political power ousted him from his place in the leadership of the Democratic party.

Bryan was also right about those "who would die" for him. Until a few days before his death he never lost his almost magical power among the people he loved—the small-town and country people of the South and West.

The most dangerous abiding trait of these people was their distrust of learning. They had reason for distrust. They were poor, and many of them had had little chance to learn. As a result, they both worshiped and feared education. Their reli-

gion was one of direct revelation. It had been that way since
the great revivals of the late eighteenth century, when only the
obsessed and dedicated Methodists and new Baptist preachers
would ride over the Allegheny Mountains, that almost impass-
able great cultural divide. These riders were the only ones who
would preach to the small-town and country people, bring
them news of the East, gather them together in the only social
life they knew—the huge camp meetings—marry them in mass
spring weddings, and say the words over all the members of
their close-knit families who had died during the winter.

In short, the circuit-riding preachers were the only ones
from outside to pay attention to the backcountry dwellers in
their wild, unbelievable isolation. In the 1920's the circuit riders' shadow still hung over these people. They explained the
name of the first tree to blossom in the spring, the "sarvice
tree," as meaning that the winter was over and that someone
would come over the mountains to see them and hold a "sarvice" over their new marriages, their new children, and their
winter dead.

What kind of man was Bryan? Theodore Roosevelt said of
him, "By George, he would make the greatest Baptist preacher
on earth." The popular press and the people referred to him as
Elijah, a second Saint Paul, a Knight in Shining Armor. He has
been called the "greatest political evangelist of his day." His
abiding weakness, shared by his followers, was a tragic, not a
vicious, one. He never asked a question. He only answered. He
believed with his heart and let his mind grow rigid.

By the 1920's, Bryan had not changed, but the times had.
And, as change often has since, it brought a shiver of fear to
the plain, unsophisticated people of America. The progress made
in science and accepted by the more modern churches meant
nothing to these people. Progress brought them no relief from
their poverty of mind or daily living. All progress seemed to be
for an elite of which these people were not a part and it

seemed to be couched in a language no one attempted to help them understand. An attitude of sharing frontier democracy was replaced by an attitude of contempt among both the intelligent and the rich. The survival of the fittest had become a social and an intellectual attitude and the common people had no defense but the past and their simple, dependable God. They needed a scapegoat. The fear words were "modernist" and "ee-volutionary," as the southern Fundamentalists pronounced it.

It was time to save America from modern ideas, city Babylons, short skirts, eastern money, atheism, and Charles Darwin.

4

The Fundamentals

At the conservative end of the vast Protestant complex of churches were the strictest Methodists and Presbyterians, frugal, stern, with all the sense-denying virtues. Conservative also, but more emotional, were the tent meetings, with their ecstasies, shouting, drama, and crowd hypnosis. Between them, these religious groups provided Bryan's Americans with their poetry, their music, their oratory, their entertainment, and their social contacts. Their meetings oiled the people's prejudices. Their preachers told followers that God loved them and not the smart-aleck Easterners. William Jennings Bryan told the people the same thing.

"It is better that we know The Rock of Ages than that we know the age of rocks," Bryan called out over and over again in tent meetings, at conventions, and at the traveling Chautauqua shows, which took education, music, and entertainment to the American people during the early years of the twentieth century.

From 1904 on, the setting up of the tent for the Chautauqua show had been one of the most familiar and exciting events in the small towns of the Midwest. Chautauqua brought culture to the intellectually starved people at the same time it employed the camp-meeting techniques they were used to. While the annual visit of the circus might be too heathen for some of the town's church people, nobody was too holy to attend Chautauqua. It combined "wholesome entertainment" with culture, health with morals. A typical program might include recitations from Shakespeare, a violin solo, a doctor lecturing on clean living, and a famous orator, or a missionary just back from saving the poor "savages."

The Chautauqua circuit provided Bryan with a perfect platform after World War I. He spoke not of politics or reform, but of the other subject nearest his heart—the simple fundamental religion that he shared with his audiences.

"Read the Bible," Hal Kimberly of the Georgia legislature said. "It teaches you how to act. Read the hymn book. It contains the finest poetry ever written. Read the almanac. It shows you how to figure out what the weather will be. There isn't another book that is necessary for anyone to read, and therefore I am opposed to all libraries."

Darwin had called his explanation of evolution only a theory. Delegates to the Niagara Bible Conference in 1896 called *their* decisions irrevocable truth, unassailable and unquestionable. The conference was attended by conservative small-town and country Christians from all over the United States. They were of all the more evangelical denominations, but they had one thing in common—fear, and the hate that always attends it. They thought that the more sophisticated clergy had deserted their faith. They had to make a clear statement, not of belief, but of easily grasped Christian truth.

Their truth came to have five parts, which were set forth in 1910 in a series of pamphlets called *The Fundamentals*. These five main parts, or fundamentals, of evangelical Christianity were, first, the infallibility, the essential factual truth, of the whole of the Bible; second, the Virgin Birth; third, Christ's Atonement; fourth, the Resurrection; fifth, the Second Coming of Christ.

There was nothing new, or even surprising, in this restatement of Christian dogma. Most of it was in the Nicene Creed, said every Sunday in the churches. The first fundamental was taught without question to children when they learned their catechism.

Tracts and pamphlets poured out from the World Christian Fundamentals Association, the Bible League of North America, the Testimony Publishing Company, the Fundamental Truth Depot, and hundreds of other publishers. The printed material blanketed the South. Once again, as in the eighteenth-century Great Revival, attention was being paid to rural America.

T. T. Martin, a revivalist, wrote *Hell and the High Schools.* Poetry was published, and learned by the children.

Evolution in "the Grades"

O, teach whate'er you will in the mighty seats
  of learning,
But fie on you that smudge the child mind's
  pure discerning.

With glib surmisings of a monkeyed ancestry's
  tail-twining
Thru million-million years of chattering,
  screeching, whining.
O, teach whate'er you will to minds less
  pure and trusting,
But from "the grades" avaunt! . . . this
  mess nausate, disgusting.

Fundamentalism, after all, touched everything a decent man stood for. Without it, as one writer warned, acceptance of the Darwinian theory would unleash "defalcations and robberies, and murders, and infanticides, and adulteries, and drunkenness, and every form and degree of social dishonor."

Darwin and the natural scientists who followed him were working on the theory that man and the lower primates had descended from a common ancestor. It was the enemies of Darwinism who said that man was descended from an ape.

In 1916, James Henry Leuba, a psychologist, published a study of the religious ideas and beliefs of college students. It was called *The Belief in God and Immortality*. It showed that there was a decided loss of faith among students from the time of entering college to the time of leaving it. Innocently, a scientific survey had provided more fuel for the Fundamentalists' fire than anything they had written themselves.

When Bryan read Leuba's book, he found a new crusade. The most popular man in America took to the speaking trail he had trod so long as a politician. The great silver voice poured out the old eloquence in a new cause—religion.

"Christ has made of death a narrow, starlit strip," he warned audience after audience, "between the companionship of yesterday and the reunion of tomorrow; evolution strikes out the stars and deepens the gloom that enshrouds the tomb. . . .

"I have no use for any man who prefers the blood of the beast to the Blood of the Lamb," he told his followers.

The function of a preacher-politician like Bryan was not to inform, but to speak words that influenced his followers to believe as he wanted them to. A close analysis of his words shows where he was leading them.

A scientific soviet is attempting to dictate what shall be taught in our schools and, in so doing, is attempting to mold the religion of the nation. It is the smallest, the most impudent, the most tyrannical oligarchy that ever attempted to exercise arbitrary power.

He had managed to equate intelligence with communism, tyranny, science, and a dangerous minority.

5 🖋

Tennessee, 1925

Bryan was not too radical to arouse love in the eastern counties of Tennessee in 1925. He was merely too Democratic to vote for. Almost solidly, the mountain counties all the way from West Virginia down through Georgia were Republican in politics and had been since before the Civil War.

"Before the War," said V. O. Key, in *Southern Politics*, "the small upland farmer constituted a class apart from the lowland planters. The yeoman of the hills was reluctant to abandon the Union for the cause of the planter and his slaves. . . . The highland yeomanry did not want to fight a rich man's war; the Democratic party was, or at least became, the planters' party and the war party. The Democratic party forced the hills into the War, and for this it has never been forgiven. There is, of course, more than the recollection of war underlying the Republicanism of the hills."

Much of "the Republicanism of the hills" can be explained in terms of topsoil. "All things come to the house downhill" is a mountain saying. Rain brings the topsoil down into the valleys to the farmer lucky enough to have inherited land in the river bottom.

There was also, and even more important, the religious difference. The valley people tended to belong to the established churches—the more progressive Presbyterians, and the Episcopalians. To the mountain people these denominations were highfalutin' and far from the passionate God who had been known to speak directly to a neighbor or a cousin right out of a tree or a cloud, as God did to Moses.

The counties of eastern Tennessee had more reason to hate the War party and the culture that went with it. They had been in the way of one of its most terrible campaigns, and even by 1925 they had not recovered from it. Within the living memory of grandparents, nearly a generation of men had been wiped out as the armies fought back and forth, up and down the lifeline of the mountains, the Tennessee River. The valley had been raked over and over by battle, by the starving, marauding troops of both sides. Here was the dreadful Chickamauga, which legend says means "river of death," where after one of the worst battles of the war, the ground had run and heaved with crawling, dying men. Towering over the rest is Lookout Mountain, watching over Chattanooga, the city that still, in 1925, showed scars of its siege. Up the Tennessee from Chattanooga stretches Missionary Ridge, and across from it, for miles up the western side of the river, runs Walden's Ridge.

Illiterate, poverty-stricken by war, the farmers of eastern Tennessee retreated farther and farther back into their rocky hillsides, scratched a living, and trusted no one. From time to time, people did come to the mountains, but they came to speculate on coal land, not to stay. They came to take and not to bring.

So the mountain people learned from their fathers, for there was no one else to learn from. They kept to the old ways, for they were too cut off to be exposed to the new. Sometimes they went down the mountain and worked in the mines, but in the early part of this century the coal business in Tennessee was speculative and physically dangerous. Wildcat mines opened. Populations grew around them. The mines closed overnight, leaving more people stranded in the narrow hollows. Sometimes the young men went to the northern cities to look for work. It was then that they found out that to the rest of the country they were a joke. They came back, hurt and bitter.

Logging companies came to lease the lands and kill the trees, exposing more of the thin, age-old topsoil of the mountains to rain and wind. When the trees were all gone, the loggers left.

Farming did not bring as much cash money, but it was dependable. So the farmers plowed the fields, the same steeply tilted fields, over and over, and planted their crops. The gulley-washing rains came and carried the exposed topsoil downhill. The bony ridges of the Alleghenies grew second-growth timber, scrub pine. The mountain people knew by experience what rock bottom meant. They were among the poorest people in the United States.

They ate sowbelly and sang old songs. They played the dulcimer, the fiddle, and the banjo. Long, long ago they had brought with them, up into the mountains, the gentle good manners of their Scottish ancestors, and also their pride. Perhaps it was this that made them able to survive. They had moved from one tragically beautiful rockbound country to another, and so they felt at home. Because they were so isolated, they founded a culture of their own. Nashville was the center of their world. From it came their music, their Bible salesmen, and very rarely, their store-bought clothes, and from time to time the wagons of the revivalists, who set up their tents in the fields and made the mountains echo with hollers and singing and speaking in unknown tongues.

6

The Butler Act

Down in the narrow valleys, where the topsoil lodged, the farmers were more prosperous. They lived a gentler life, not different in kind, but different in harshness from that of their mountain kin. A few more inches of topsoil meant a good dependable crop, some money in the bank, maybe a boy or girl in college.

John Washington Butler, from Macon County, Tennessee, was one of these farmers. By Macon County standards, his farm was large—one hundred and twenty acres. His great-grandfather, his grandfather, and his father had worked it. When he was twenty-one, he took it over.

Butler was well liked in his neighborhood. He was a tall, broad-shouldered farmer with a face tanned by the weather, and a big, ready smile. As the years passed, he and his wife raised a family that remained a close one. When his daughters married, they stayed in the county. His three teen-age boys, with their uncle and their cousin, made up a family brass band.

Butler was a credit to his community. Every Sunday he

went into the county seat of Lafayette and attended church. He served as clerk of the Round Lick Association of Primitive Baptists. He was a schoolmaster for five years, teaching in the fall and planting his crops in the spring. That was the kind of service a good man gave to his neighbors. It is no wonder that he was asked to run for the state legislature.

One of the promises he made the voters was to do something about the ungodly teaching of evolution in the public schools.

"In the first place," he said, "the Bible is the foundation upon which our American government is built, and the teaching of anything which denies the Bible will, I believe, destroy the principles which have made our nation what it is. . . . The evolutionist who denies the Biblical story of creation, as well as other Biblical accounts, cannot be a Christian. . . . It goes hand in hand with modernism, makes Jesus Christ a fakir, robs the Christian of his hope, and undermines the foundation of our government. . . ."

During his first term in the state legislature, Butler was too shy to introduce a bill outlawing the teaching of evolution, but in 1925, during his second term, on the morning of his forty-ninth birthday, he finally got up the nerve to do it. He sat down and wrote out a bill.

An Act prohibiting the teaching of the Evolution Theory in all the Universities, Normals and all other public schools of Tennessee, which are supported in whole or in part by the public school funds of the State, and to provide penalties for the violations thereof.

Section 1. Be it enacted by the General Assembly of the State of Tennessee, That it shall be unlawful for any teacher in any of the Universities, Normals and all other public schools of the State which are supported in whole or in part by the public school funds of the State, to teach any theory that denies the story of the Divine Creation of man as taught in the Bible, and to teach instead that man has descended from a lower order of animals.

Section 2. Be it further enacted, That any teacher found guilty of the violation of this Act shall be guilty of a misdemeanor and upon conviction, shall be fined not less than One Hundred ($100.00) Dollars nor more than Five Hundred ($500.00) Dollars for each offense.

Later he said, "If I had to do it all over again I'd have introduced it two years earlier—in my first term in the legislature. I didn't know anything about evolution when I introduced it. I'd read in the papers that boys and girls were coming home from school and telling their fathers and mothers that the Bible was all nonsense. I didn't think that was right, and then the Reverend W. J. Murray of Nashville, who comes to preach once a month at our church in Lafayette, the Primitive Baptist Church, came over one Sunday and preached a sermon saying the teaching of evolution in the schools ought to be stopped, because it was attacking religion. When the bill passed, I naturally thought we wouldn't hear any more about evolution in Tennessee."

Butler's act passed because of a series of political expediencies, accidents, and social habits. The house of representatives let it go through by a vote of 71 to 5 because they did not want to offend the Fundamentalists in their backcountry counties. When the act went to the senate, only two members had the courage to speak out against it. The speaker of the upper house rose. He called out, "Save our children for God!" The senate passed the act, 24 to 6. Most of the members expected Governor Peay to veto it.

When Governor Peay signed the act instead, he was heard

to mutter, "They've got their nerve to pass the buck to me when they know I want to be United States senator."

Governor Peay had better reasons than his own ambitions for signing the act. He was an ardent advocate of improving the school system in Tennessee, already shamefully behind the rest of the country. It was hard to persuade the representatives of poor farmers who were illiterate that they ought to pay higher taxes out of their already meager cash incomes to give their children free and extended education. As it was, the governor was only fighting to lengthen the school year to eight months. He would not have dared to go to the legislature and ask for money to do it if he had gone so against public opinion as to veto the Butler Act.

Besides, no one thought the act mattered. It was, in the cynical terms of state politics, a sop to the naïve voter. The valley men in the legislature were doing to the simple backcountry people what had always been done to them—city things, courting citizens for their vote instead of taking on the more formidable and responsible task of helping them to open their starved minds.

Later a Tennessee lawyer said, "The legislature did not know it passed the fool thing."

The problem of why there was so little opposition to the act from either educators or the press was more complicated than simply one of money for the schools. Already six professors at the state university had been fired from their jobs over differences with the Fundamentalists. One of the professors was the dean of the law school, John Randolph Neal. The president of the University of Tennessee knew that the legislature watched his every move.

But the reason there was so little opposition ran deeper than that—as deep as the Tennessee River and as old as the coming of the first white man across the mountains. The reason was the mountain local pride and fear of ridicule—protection of one's own against the outsiders, the exploiters, the ones who have never understood and never will understand. Tennessee liberals might ridicule and condemn the bill themselves and tell stories to each other about mountain credulity and mountain sagacity, but they deeply resented the exposure of their culture to the shallow, quick-thinking world outside their valleys. No matter how intelligent they are, people of mountain blood make good poets, good preachers, sometimes good lawyers, but they do not make good logicians, empiricists, or administrators. Their passions and their anger run too deep.

So they spoke among themselves, sitting around arguing in the local newspaper office, the barbershop, the drugstore, the ice-cream parlor, but the arguments did not cross the state line. Even the local newspapers hardly mentioned the Butler Act.

7

The American Civil Liberties Union

By 1925, the Fundamentalists had already succeeded in getting teachers fired from their jobs and had embarrassed liberal ministers all over the southern states. The Fundamentalists' pressure had not been great enough to get an actual law against the teaching of evolution passed, but since 1923 their influence had been responsible for the issuing of temporary orders by officials to ban such teaching in Florida, Oklahoma, North Carolina, and Texas. The Fundamentalists had tried to get a law through in Kentucky, but it had failed, mostly because the liberals at the university had had the courage to speak out against it.

But now, at last, there was a law against the dreaded scientific theory that denied the Bible. Although Butler had introduced the bill on his own, he became a Fundamentalist hero. There was a rumor, which was not true, that William Jennings Bryan had written the act for him.

Although they did not know it, the Fundamentalists were running up against a centuries-old quarrel—one that had separated church and state, had formed the basis of their country's political philosophy, and had even put the Bible they swore by into their hands.

The battle had been fought ever since Galileo looked up through his telescope and saw the stars, and for his work was arrested by the Inquisition in Rome in 1633. No one thought to tell the Fundamentalists the history of courage and revolt in the face of just the kind of dogmatism they were seeking to impose. It had been forgotten that John Wycliffe, the fourteenth-century English clergyman, had fought all his life so that their ancestors could read the Bible in their own vulgar language instead of the secret and aristocratic language, Latin. Wycliffe's body had been dug up after his death and had been publicly burned as a warning to other heretics.

The Fundamentalists' very political philosophy—of individualism, of neighborly help, of democracy itself—and their extreme Puritan religion came from such men as John Lilburne, the seventeenth-century Puritan martyr who was whipped through the streets of London, preaching as the cart pulled him along, until he was gagged to keep him from speaking out against what he called the enemies of Christ.

It was John Lilburne who had said:

> For what is done to any one may be done to every one: besides, being all members of one body, that is, of the English Commonwealth, one man should not suffer wrongfully, but all should be sensible, and endeavour his preservation; otherwise they give way to an inlet of the sea of will and power, upon their laws and liberties, which are the boundaries to keep out tyranny and oppression; and who assists not in such cases, betrays his own rights, and is overrun, and of a free man made a slave when he thinks not of it, or regards it not, and so shunning the censure of turbulency, incurs the guilt of treachery to the present and future generations.

The "future generations" who still lived by many of Lilburne's reforms had forgotten his name; not so a group of Americans who started an organization called the American Civil Liberties Union. They used John Lilburne's saying as their watchword.

The union was started during World War I to defend pacifists who were arrested for refusing to fight, for reasons of conscience. It carried on afterward for the more general purpose of legally defending anyone the union thought was being deprived of the liberties guaranteed Americans under the Bill of Rights.

One of the ACLU's directors was Jane Addams, an outstanding woman of the time, who had founded Hull House, the first American slum settlement for social work in Chicago. Another was Helen Keller, the blind, deaf and dumb woman who was already a living legend. Lawyers all over the country subscribed to the ACLU: John W. Davis, who had run for President on the Democratic ticket in 1924; Charles Evans Hughes and Felix Frankfurter, later of the Supreme Court; Arthur Garfield Hays, Dudley Field Malone, and Clarence Darrow, all nationally known attorneys.

Lucile Milner was the secretary of the union in 1925. One of her jobs was to make newspaper clippings, either of cases that might need the defense of a Civil Liberties lawyer or of items that might have to do with the essential reasons for the existence of the organization. In a Tennessee paper she came upon a small item about the passage of the Butler Act. To the dedicated people of the American Civil Liberties Union such a story was like an alarm bell. The Butler Act, to them, put chains of tradition on the human mind, negated the right of free speech, and fettered the teaching profession.

They thought that what was being done to the teachers in Tennessee could be "done to every one," could spread like forest fire until the freedom of the American mind to think and to explore, indeed even to doubt, could be as circumscribed as once Galileo's had been, or Wycliffe's, or John Lilburne's. Members of the board of the American Civil Liberties Union decided to act. They sent a press release to the Tennessee papers saying that if any teacher would agree to let himself be arrested under the act, they would provide financial support, publicity, and the best legal defense in the country. The statement appeared in the *Chattanooga News* on the afternoon of May 4, 1925.

8 ✍

Dayton and Scopes

Every leading citizen of the town of Dayton, Tennessee, met to drink chocolate sodas, lemon phosphates, or other delicacies from the soda fountain in Robinson's drugstore. They reared back on the wire ice-cream chairs in the shade and listened to the slow creak of the big iron ceiling fans, the soda spurting into ice-cream drinks at the fountain, and the sound of each other's voices. Across the street stretched the spacious two-acre courthouse lawn. Nothing moved under its maple trees and its water oaks. The weather was already too hot in May for anything much to move around in midafternoon. Once in a while, a black Model T Ford passed at the town speed limit, twelve miles an hour, down one of the two seamed concrete streets under the trees. There were a few Chandler sedans and a Packard in the town, but most of the cars were Model T's. From time to time a wagon or a buckboard from one of the farms moved slowly past the screen door of the drugstore. Everybody knew who everybody was, in the way of small towns.

There wasn't much to do in Dayton. A man was thrown

back on his intelligence, his prejudices, or bootleg liquor, of which there was a plentiful supply up in the gaps of Walden's Ridge, the long mountain that looked down over the town and almost seemed to protect it. There was a moving-picture show, an old clay tennis court, and a swimming hole not far out of town, up Richland Creek. Dayton had a golf club. There were box suppers at the churches, for the "nice" people, and once in a great while, for people farther down the social scale, there were hot gospel revival meetings on the edge of town. At Morgan Springs, up on top of Walden's Ridge, dances were held on Saturday night, and all of what Dayton called the younger set went there on dates, to dance, and to spoon. There were girls with names like Rose and Opal, Lily and Pearl—small-town names in the fashion of the new century. They danced to "Lady, Be Good" and "Yes, Sir, That's My Baby."

People went thirty-eight miles to Chattanooga to shop. There were several trains a day, but most of them whistled and rushed past Dayton.

The real center of the town was Robinson's drugstore. It wasn't much to look at. There were lots of advertisements on the windows, and patent medicines inside them; then at the back, out of the way of the sun, were the soda fountain and the ice-cream chairs, around the little round drugstore tables on their wrought-iron bases.

George W. Rappelyea was an outsider, even though he was married to a girl from Rhea County. In the first place, he was from New York. In the second place, although he was superintendent of the Sunday school at the Five Points Methodist Episcopal Church, he was what Tennesseans called an out-and-out arguing, hollering "eevolutionist."

Evolution was a subject on everybody's mind in the spring of 1925. Little boys ran through the school yard teasing each other with the chant, "Your old man's a monkey!"

George Rappelyea had a greater concern than monkeys. All

through the mountain region the coal mines were catching the first whiff of what was later to be a worldwide depression. In the language of the region, "the bottom was dropping out of the coal business." Rappelyea saw a chance to attract some northern money to the district. It was needed, for no matter how greatly "outside" money was resented once it arrived, much of the business energy in the South went into attracting it.

Rappelyea was a live wire. He was always thinking up schemes to improve Dayton, to open up the defunct iron mines and put Dayton back on the map, as it had been in the 1870's, when the mines were working full time and the population was swelled to four thousand by the miners who were transported from Scotland to work them. In 1925, the population was only eighteen hundred people.

The other men who dropped into Robinson's were as much a part of the town as the water oaks on the courthouse lawn. Sue Hicks, one of three brothers, was a lawyer. So was Wallace Haggard, the son of A. P. Haggard, the local mayor, bank president, and factory owner. His enemies said A. P. Haggard owned Dayton; his admirers said he had done a lot for it. Doc Robinson, the druggist, usually joined in whatever discussion had taken over the afternoon. He was married to A. P. Haggard's sister. Then there was Walter White, the Rhea County superintendent of schools.

On the warm afternoon of Tuesday, May 5, the argument was fierce. Rappelyea had read the day before that the American Civil Liberties Union was willing to pay for a test case against the Butler Act in Tennessee. He came to the drugstore with one of his plans in mind to, in his own words, "put Dayton on the map."

It was easy to get tempers hot. Both Wallace Haggard and Hicks were against evolution, but not rabidly, as the Fundamentalists were. Socially and culturally, neither man was the kind to ally himself with extremists, but they argued against Rappelyea in favor of the Butler Act. It is easy to suspect that at that point their stand on the act was just for the sake of argument on a spring afternoon.

At the right place in the discussion, Rappelyea said they ought to test the case in Dayton. Finally he persuaded the others. There was only one thing wrong with the idea. On the Friday before, school had finished for the summer. But somebody remembered that the new young science teacher was still in town.

A boy was sitting up at the fountain drinking a soda through a straw. "Go find the professor and tell him to come on down here. We want to talk to him," someone called to him. The boy finished his soda and ran off down the street into the sun.

Ever since he had arrived in Dayton the fall before, John Scopes had been trying to break people of calling him "the professor."

9 🖋

The Infidel Scopes

It was only by accident that John Scopes was still in Dayton. He had planned to go back to Paducah, Kentucky, where his family lived, and take a summer job. He was twenty-four years old and earned $150 a month teaching science and coaching the high-school football team. Both the teaching job and the summer job selling Fords were ways of making enough money so that he could go to graduate school.

He had enjoyed his four days of holiday. It was warm enough to go to the swimming hole. A friend had lent him a little yellow Dodge roadster to run around in. It was a good Tuesday at the end of a good year and he had to admit he was still hanging around town because he wanted to take a pretty girl he had just met to a box supper at the church.

On that afternoon he was playing tennis on the old clay court at the high school. In the middle of the game he noticed a little boy waiting on the sidelines and watching the ball being batted back and forth. At the end of the volley the boy told John Scopes some men wanted to see him down at Robin-

John T. Scopes in June, 1925. (PHOTO FROM THE BETTMANN ARCHIVE)

son's drugstore. Scopes walked the three-quarters of a mile along the shaded, sand-covered street, not even bothering to change his sweaty clothes. He was in no hurry. Doc Robinson was chairman of the Rhea County school board. Scopes thought he wanted to talk about some leftover school business.

John Scopes enjoyed Dayton. People had been nice to him. He boarded at the house of Mr. Bailey, who owned the hardware store. Scopes knew all the young people in town. He was the youngest and most popular teacher in the Rhea County Central High School.

Some of the most rock-ribbed Fundamentalists did not approve of him. They thought him a rather outspoken young whippersnapper; besides, there was a rumor around that he smoked, courted the girls on the porch swings, never missed a dance at Morgan Springs, and even, once in a while, drank a little bootleg liquor. He went to church every Sunday, but that did not keep him from being an outspoken "eevolutionist." Not exactly outspoken—the slim, blond Scopes was too shy for that—but he knew his own mind and he did not mind speaking it. Most people thought him a popular young man, quiet, genial, and attractive.

When he got to Robinson's drugstore, he knew everybody there. He sat down while the boy behind the fountain made him a soda.

"John, we've been arguing," Rappelyea told him, "and I said that nobody could teach biology without teaching evolution."

John Scopes agreed with him, as he had many times before in the same argument. He went further. A book called *Civic Biology*, by George William Hunter, was sitting on a nearby shelf among the textbooks that the drugstore supplied. It had been used officially by Tennessee schools since 1919. It contained a résumé of the Darwinian theory. John Scopes showed it to the men and laughed. The Butler Act had not mentioned the fact that evolution had been approved for the public schools for some years.

"You have been teaching 'em this book?" Rappelyea asked.

John Scopes said he had, but only by chance. He was not the official biology teacher, but he had substituted for the regular teacher for two weeks in the spring, and he had reviewed the whole term's work for the final examinations. He supposed he had included evolution.

"Then you've been violating the law," said Doc Robinson. Robinson handed Scopes the *Chattanooga News* item placed by the American Civil Liberties Union.

"John," he said, "would you be willing to stand for a test case?"

John Scopes did not like the idea of an arrest and all the publicity that would go with it. But Rappelyea kept at him and finally Scopes consented. He said afterward, "I realized that the best time to scotch the snake is when it starts to wiggle. The snake already had been wiggling a good, long time." He knew that someone had to stand up to the stifling of freedom that could be the result of enforcing the Butler Act.

He agreed to stand trial.

Robinson walked over to the wall telephone, cranked the bell, and told Central to get him the city desk at the *Chattanooga News*.

"This is F. E. Robinson in Dayton," he said. "I'm chairman of the school board here. We've just arrested a man for teaching evolution."

Rappelyea's plan for putting Dayton on the map had been put in motion.

John Scopes drank his soda and went on back to the high-school court to finish his tennis game. No one seemed to consider that he had taken an extremely dangerous step. Among the ridges of eastern Tennessee, people had been shot for a lot less than he was doing.

10 ✐

Clarence Darrow

John Scopes was not fated to sell Fords in Paducah, Kentucky, that summer. Three days after the telephone call to the *Chattanooga News,* the arrest story was worldwide. Hurriedly, Judge John Tate Raulston called a special grand jury to indict Scopes. There was danger that some other Tennessee town would steal the publicity by bringing someone to trial before Dayton could. The judge set a special trial date for July 10.

In 1923, one of the country's best-known lawyers, Clarence Darrow, had written that "man is the product of heredity and environment and that he acts as his machine responds to outside stimuli and nothing else seems amply proven by the evolution and history of man. . . . This is not a universe where acts result from chance. Law is everywhere."

In 1924, Darrow, best known as a labor lawyer, had saved the lives of two teen-age murderers, Richard Loeb and Nathan Leopold, on just these ideas—that man's heredity and environment are overwhelmingly decisive factors in his acts. The case had made him famous—even notorious—throughout the country.

No three men ever bore out what Darrow said better than the leading actors in the trial that followed John Scopes's arrest.

Scopes had been taught to think for himself, to read what he wanted, to stand up for what he believed, by his father, Thomas Scopes. The elder Scopes was a railroad machinist, a local union leader, and a follower of Eugene Debs, who had been head of the American Railway Union. Thomas Scopes had come from England in 1885 as a very young man. He had been born a Cockney in London, where a boy learned to fight early for what he believed in. There he had already served his apprenticeship, both as a machinist and as a strong trade unionist. He had married into a sturdy Presbyterian family in Kentucky. When John was a child, the family had moved from Kentucky to Illinois and back to Kentucky again, always with the new and booming railroads. Thomas Scopes's union-organizing kept him in trouble. Company after company blacklisted him for it. In 1922 his union went on strike against the Chicago and Eastern Illinois Railroad. As a result of that strike he never worked again.

Thomas Scopes was an almost completely self-educated man. Around the fire at night he read to John and his sisters—books by Ruskin, Macaulay, Carlyle, Mark Twain, Dickens, and Charles Darwin. John Scopes heard *The Origin of Species*, *The Descent of Man*, and *The Voyage of the Beagle* in his father's voice.

John Scopes had, in a way, been trained all his life to have the courage to agree to his arrest.

William Jennings Bryan was in the middle of one of his beloved cross-country Fundamentalist speaking tours when he heard of Scopes's arrest. He reacted with all the force of a whole lifetime of belief, lecturing, Fundamentalist study, and propaganda.

On May 13, Bryan wired William B. Riley's World's Christian Fundamentals Association that he would act as counsel in the case of the State of Tennessee v. John T. Scopes. That evening, speaking to the Interdenominational Conference on Fundamentals in West Chester, Pennsylvania, Bryan gave his reasons:

This is a matter for the nation. It is one of the greatest questions ever raised, the question of the right of the people who created and support the schools to control them. If not they—then who?

The Fundamentalists are trying to establish the doctrine [that] the taxpayers have a right to say what shall be taught—the taxpayers and not the scientists.

There are only eleven thousand members of the American Association for the Advancement of Science. I don't believe one in ten thousand should dictate to the rest of us. Can a handful of scientists rob your children of religion and turn them out atheists? We'll find 109 million Americans on the other side. For the first time in my life I'm on the side of the majority.

When the word got back to Dayton that Bryan would act as counsel for the prosecution, Rappelyea, the publicity mastermind, was delighted. It had been part of the plan born in the drugstore to get as many famous men as possible to take part in the trial.

Although Tennessee law provided for the trying of cases by prominent attorneys from outside the state if there was a member of the Tennessee bar on the case as well, few outside lawyers had actually been called in, and never on such a minor breach of the law. As one Tennessee lawyer said, "What business do you think William Jennings Bryan, who has not tried a lawsuit in twenty-five years, has coming here to assist the bench and bar of Tennessee in the trial of a little misdemeanor case that any judge ought to be able to dispose of in a couple of hours?"

Actually, it was nearly forty years since sixty-five-year-old Bryan had had his brief day as a courtroom lawyer. The "little misdemeanor" was his great last chance to defend his beloved Bible against the infidels and regain his place as the leading American champion of the neglected and forgotten.

The trial came at exactly the right time for him. In the face of his defeats, he still had not given up his political hopes. He had bought a home in Florida and it was rumored that he had established residence in the southern state in order to run for the United States Senate. In April, 1925, Bryan wrote to Edward Keating, a newspaper editor in Washington, "the term in the Senate would enable me to help lay the foundations for the next Presidential campaign."

Every Sunday at noon, Bryan held an outdoor Sunday school class under the Florida palm trees, for his neighbors and usually a small crowd of tourists. He talked about the fundamentals of Christianity, and sometimes about Florida real estate.

John Scopes was sick with embarrassment about the trial. He had thought it was to be a local case—a case among friends to prove a point that to him was one of honor. The thing that bothered him as well was that he could not exactly remember having mentioned Darwin during his two weeks as a biology substitute. He talked things over with his father. The old fighter told him that he had been given a great chance to serve his country.

Hesitant, shy, and abashed, young John Thomas Scopes walked into the national limelight and into a quarrel years older than he was. He did not even have a lawyer.

This situation was not to last long.

The same morning that Bryan accepted the case, a man sent word from the Hotel Aqua, Dayton's one hotel, that he wanted to talk to John Scopes. He offered himself as Scopes's attorney.

He was John Randolph Neal, the ex-dean of the law school at the University of Tennessee, one of the first victims in the Fundamentalist campaign against learning.

On the same night that Bryan threw down the gauntlet in West Chester, Clarence Darrow was speaking to the American Psychiatric Association on "The Sane Treatment of Crime" in Richmond, Virginia.

If, by all Darrow's theories, William Jennings Bryan and John Scopes had been cast for their roles in the trial, even more so had Darrow himself. He had grown up in Kinsman, Ohio, a town less than half the size of Dayton.

Clarence Darrow had been born thumping a cracker barrel. His gentle and deeply sincere father, Amirus, had been trained as a minister, but had lost his faith—or had gained a sense of intellectual questioning and doubt new and rare to the simple thinking of men in the nineteenth century. He was dirt poor, and the best-educated man for miles around. Clarence Darrow grew up seeing this man whom he adored scratch a living as a furniture maker and undertaker in a town that had made him into the local eccentric because of his beliefs.

Like Scopes, Darrow and his six brothers and sisters were educated by their father, who read to them everything that the mid-nineteenth century had to offer to stretch their growing minds. Clarence Darrow grew up defending, first with his fists and later with words, the honor of the intellectual minority in a small town of simple people. The intellectual minority was his own family. By the time he was eighteen, when he took a job teaching school at thirty dollars a month, he argued as easily as he breathed. In those days, Saturday-night debates on any subject the opponents could decide on were a fixed entertainment before the square dances. Darrow loved to take part in both the arguments and the dancing. He would debate the other side of any subject and for the rest of the evening would have a great time swinging his partner to the sound of the fiddle.

At sixty-eight, Darrow still had his youthful zest for life, for argument, for healthy, demanding doubt, and for free and open education. He had one blind spot—the Fundamentalists. All his life, in one way or another, he had fought them and the past they wanted to turn back to. He believed in and defended the idea of the future, of progress. In his defense of Loeb and Leopold he had said:

> I am not pleading so much for these boys as I am for the infinite number of others to follow, those who perhaps cannot be as well defended as these have been, those who may go down in the tempest without aid. It is of them I am thinking and for them I am begging of this court not to turn backward toward the barbarous and cruel past.

It was the "barbarous and cruel past" that Darrow volunteered once again to fight against. He was partly persuaded by the leading intellectual hornet of the country, H. L. Mencken.

Mencken had already given names to the trial and the place. Henceforth the court proceedings would be referred to as the Monkey Trial, and that part of America where they took place would be called the Bible Belt.

"Nobody gives a damn about that yap schoolteacher," Mencken told Darrow. "The thing to do is to make a fool out of Bryan."

From Richmond, Darrow sent a telegram offering his services to John Scopes as his defense attorney. He also had some questions he had been waiting for three years to ask Bryan.

In years past, their reforming zeal had made Bryan and

Clarence Darrow at Dayton, Tennessee, in 1925. (PHOTO FROM THE BETTMANN ARCHIVE)

Darrow friends. Darrow had twice campaigned for Bryan for the presidency; but in later years, when Bryan had taken up the white banner of Fundamentalism, Darrow had drawn back in some contempt. In 1923, Darrow had publicly sent a list of fifty-five questions to Bryan, in a highly publicized campaign by the Fundamentalists against the teaching of evolution. They were, Darrow said, "a few questions to Mr. Bryan and the Fundamentalists, [which] if fairly answered, might serve the interests of reaching the truth—all of this assuming that truth is desirable."

Darrow asked, among other things, how the serpent traveled before he tempted Eve and was cursed by having to crawl on his belly; how old the earth was; whether Bryan thought God made the earth in six days exactly.

Bryan had ignored the questions.

Darrow decided to go to Dayton to ask them again.

There was trouble with the American Civil Liberties Union. The more conservative members thought Darrow and the man he had chosen to go with him, Dudley Field Malone, were too flamboyant. They wanted less colorful and more respectable lawyers. They were afraid of turning the trial into a circus. After all, Malone had attracted publicity by his radical actions, and the ACLU shrank from any taint of radicalism. Malone had resigned from the State Department, where he had served under Bryan, but he had resigned for a far less popular reason than Bryan's—woman suffrage. Malone was also a Catholic who had gotten a divorce and married one of the suffragette leaders, Doris Stevens. She would not wear a wedding ring or use her "married name." She belonged to the Lucy Stone League, which disapproved of the slavery of women implied in the taking of a husband's name.

John Scopes and John Randolph Neal went to New York for conferences with the ACLU. Almost as an afterthought, Scopes was asked who he wanted to defend him. He pointed out that

John T. Scopes with some of his advisers and attorneys at Dayton, Tennessee. Left to right, in front: Clarence Darrow, Dudley Field Malone, John Randolph Neal, John T. Scopes. (UNITED PRESS INTER-NATIONAL PHOTO)

with the acceptance of William Jennings Bryan, the trial had already become a free-for-all. He said he needed a "slugger."

"I want Darrow," said Scopes. As in the rest of the trial, he spoke little, but when he did, he meant it. He was a twenty-four-year-old schoolteacher just graduated from college, and the aging giants were collecting around him. If anyone had noticed, they would have seen that under the fine red-blond hair and the freckles, his eyes were determined. He had the strong chin of his father. But already no one was noticing. The big guns were being wheeled up; the ballyhoo was beginning. Rappelyea was running the show.

It was hardly noticed when Scopes's sister lost her job as a schoolteacher because she refused to denounce her brother publicly.

Darrow, Malone, and one of the keenest legal minds in America, Arthur Garfield Hays, became Scopes's defense attorneys. The ACLU appointed John Randolph Neal as chief counsel for the defense, to comply with the Tennessee law saying that the leading counsel had to be a member of the Tennessee bar.

It was rumored that Bryan had already started writing what he hoped would be the greatest speech in a great career.

Scopes had to rush back to Dayton. Somebody had been shot at in a quarrel in the barbershop. It made a good "backwoods" story for the newspapers. When he arrived in Dayton, he found that the shooting had been staged with blanks as a publicity stunt. It was the only time in the whole summer's ordeal that he showed anger. It is not known what he said to Rappelyea, but there were no more such stunts—at least by Dayton people.

11

Apes and God

On Saturday, the Fourth of July, Dayton did not have the speechmaking and picnicking that customarily took place in small towns on Independence Day. Everybody was worried. People stood in little knots on the street corners, discussing the case and waiting for news.

Clarence Darrow, on the advice of the ACLU, was trying to get the trial changed from Dayton to a place where it could be heard away from the already growing circus atmosphere.

By July, everybody in the town had a stake in the trial. New paint had been ordered, and camp chairs and extra food. New telephone lines had been laid, houses spruced up. Dayton was ready to entertain the world if it wanted to come. Everyone in town waited all weekend for the decision that could mean the trial had been moved.

At eight o'clock on Monday night the news was chalked up on the window of Robinson's drugstore. The application to hear the case in a different court had been turned down. The preparations for the trial went on. The Hotel Aqua was painted a wild yellow. Room prices went up to eight dollars a day. Cots were put up in all the corridors. Bailey's roominghouse was already full. Outside the town, Rappelyea had hurriedly renovated an old frame building that had been a clubhouse for one of the defunct coal companies. People called it the Mansion. It was to house the expert witnesses called by the defense. Twenty-two Western Union operators were being installed in a room off the grocery store. A room for the press was set up over Bailey's hardware store. The large courtroom was painted and polished. Extra spittoons were ordered. The new inventions, microphones, were being installed. This trial was to be the first in history to be broadcast all over the country.

Already reporters from the great cities, from as far away as London, were flowing into Dayton; over a hundred newsmen were to file as many as 150,000 words a day. Partly because of the local color and partly because in 1925 it was almost unbelievable that the twentieth century would witness a man being tried in a court of law for his right as a teacher to challenge and inform, the international press headlined even the most minor events in Dayton.

Today, after the book-burnings in Germany, the suppression of dissent among writers and artists in Russia, and the anti-intellectual witch-hunts in the schools and libraries of the United States since World War II, it is just as hard to believe that so much worldwide passion could have been aroused over the trial of one twenty-four-year-old high-school teacher. In Berlin in 1925, Albert Einstein warned, "Any restriction of academic liberty heaps coals of shame upon the community which tolerates such suppression." A few years later, he would have to flee for his life from Germany because he was a Jew. In England, George Bernard Shaw said of the Scopes trial, "Monstrous nonsense."

Dayton waited in the flat, breathless calm of the river valley for the trial to begin. The open-air tabernacles set up for revivals drooped dusty and hell-hot inside.

Dayton was being turned into a carnival of monkey jokes and revivalists. There were cotton apes, and pins that read, "Your old man's a monkey." Robinson's drugstore sold monkey watch fobs and a "monkey fizz." Reporters greeted each other with the password, "Brother, thy tail hangs down behind." The only mention of Darwin was J. W. Darwin's Ready-to-Wear. A large sign over the front of the store said DARWIN IS RIGHT— *Inside.* Some circus people brought real, performing chimpanzees and set up a sideshow.

The population of the town had already tripled. Every sleeping space was taken. One policeman, Mansfield, had managed to control Dayton's torpid crime rate; now four more policemen were borrowed from Chattanooga.

All down the two main streets, refreshment stands sprouted, selling hot dogs, watermelons, ice cream, Coca-Cola, corn bread, hot biscuits. Robinson's drugstore remained the center of it all. A roaring trade was carried on at its Simian Soda Fountain. Its front window became the central news bulletin.

Fischer's Ice Cream Parlor imported a band. Two tent shows arrived. A truck was driven slowly back and forth through the town, advertising a picture show, *The Life of Christ.* Winking electric signs on the truck promised the Crucifixion, the Ascension, and the Resurrection.

By coincidence, a Holy Roller convention had been scheduled for the same week. The town was full of traveling preachers. T. T. Martin, the white-haired, genial writer of the great backcountry best seller *Hell and the High Schools,* set up shop and announced he was going to convert H. L. Mencken. One preacher called himself John the Baptist the Third; another, the Bible Champion of the World. Every night the moan of the Holy Rollers was heard, mixed with the throb of dance-band music. In the dark, the lights shone from opened windows and doors. If it was dog-day hot in the Tennessee Valley, the night

At the headquarters of T. T. Martin in Dayton, antievolution books, including writings by William Jennings Bryan, were announced on large posters and had a record sale. (BROWN BROTHERS PHOTO)

was little cooler. The porch swings sighed on the dim porches, and the palm-leaf fans fluttered as people tried to find a little relief.

A mountain woman looked at the whole thing, gathered up her brood of children, and headed for the hills. She told the reporter from the *Shreveport Times:*

All this stuff about monkeys shows the mark of the beast is on 'em and something's bound to happen. They'll go down to the lake of fire that's Hell. I ain't got no business at this here trial. I'm going to stay away, for something may happen to the courthouse. It's the Bible being fulfilled. Christ is coming to earth in a cloud from Heaven, and then after a thousand years the world will come to an end. It's all written in the Book.

To her and to thousands like her, there had been but two books for the home. One was the Bible, and the other the Sears, Roebuck catalog.

John Scopes rode his father around in his little borrowed Dodge. He was still worried, even though he was managing to enjoy himself.

One member of the grand jury that had made the formal indictment said Scopes ought to be hanged, while the foreman, John Rose, spoke the kind of quiet, thoughtful sense that the public tended to ignore as not being sensational enough: "This hellfire and brimstone stuff is all bosh. I tell my Sunday school class so. Not half of the preachers who rant about the lake of fire believe it themselves. They preach about it because it's their bread and butter. . . . When I was a boy, the Irish potato was called the London Lady and was never larger than a hen's egg. The tomato was a little, ridgy, one-sided thing that no more resembled the Ponderosa of today than a two-cylinder automobile looks like a Rolls-Royce. The cow was a crumply-

horned animal that gave about half a gallon of milk a day the
three months she wasn't dry—and the milk wasn't as good as
that we feed our hogs today. And the razor-back hog looked
like a hound dog. Stand beside our current Poland China
[hog]—then ask me if I believe in evolution."

12

Defender of the Faith

On Tuesday afternoon, the *Royal Palm* from Florida steamed into the whistle-stop station, bringing the idol of the hill country, William Jennings Bryan. The Bryan whom people—and their fathers and their grandfathers—remembered had been one of the handsomest of American statesmen, with the kind of strong jaw, piercing eyes, and long, sweeping hair that made leading movie actors of the time into popular idols.

The man who got off the train had vague traces of the young reformer. He was sixty-five years old. Defeat, age, and heavy eating had taken their toll. He looked mangy—not fat, but pale and a little scraggly. His mouth had become a wide, thin line, and his smile was by then a soft, apologetic mannerism. He was a caricature of a backcountry politician, with his pin-striped trousers, his black coat, and even a funny hat he had picked up in Panama. It was a pith sun helmet. No one in Dayton had ever seen one before. The whole town was out to meet him—except for the high-school band. John Scopes was so popular with them that no one dared to let them play for the arrival of the prosecution; people feared a noisy practical joke.

With the arrival of Bryan the town seemed to realize the solemnity of the occasion. He reminded them at a banquet given in his honor that night at the Hotel Aqua:

> What is the secret of the world's interest in this little case? It is found in the fact that this trial uncovers an attack which for a generation has been made more or less secretly upon revealed religion, that is, the Christian religion.
>
> If evolution wins, Christianity goes. Not suddenly, of course, but gradually, for the two cannot stand together. They are as antagonistic as light and darkness; as antagonistic as good and evil.

His voice was nearly as good as ever.

His arrival was the signal for the holy sign painters. With whitewash, they decorated cliffs, barn sides, trees, even the new planks on the courthouse lawn that protected the temporary sewer pipes put down for the occasion and left in gaping trenches.

Huge messages read, PREPARE TO MEET THY GOD!—SWEETHEARTS, COME TO JESUS!—JESUS IS COMING. ARE YOU READY?—YOU NEED GOD IN YOUR BUSINESS!—WHERE WILL YOU SPEND ETERNITY?

Gradually Dayton went back to the carnival atmosphere and Bryan joined it. A truck drove around Dayton advertising Florida real estate. If George Rappelyea had managed to attract any northern coal money to Rhea County, Bryan wanted to charm it on down to the Florida real-estate boom.

The most popular evangelist in the country, Billy Sunday, sent advice to Bryan. From California, Aimee Semple McPherson, the most flamboyant woman preacher in the whole popular religious movement, joined in with a telegram from her Angelus Temple in Los Angeles:

Ten thousand members of Angelus Temple with her missions of radio church membership send grateful appreciation of your lion-hearted championship of the Bible against evolution and throw our hats in the ring with you for God and the Bible as is. Constant prayer during week all night prayer Saturday night. Sunday afternoon Bible parade mass meeting and trial with hanging and burial of monkey teachers. Tennessee can count on us.

The agnostic Darrow strolled around Dayton having a fine time, as if every day he had spent out of an American small town had been a wasted one. He slung his coat over his arm, loosened his tie, bought hot dogs from the stands, and made friends with everyone.

On the same Tuesday, his first day in Dayton, H. L. Mencken, the leading American smart-aleck, sat down to give his first impressions of the town. He wrote:

The town, I confess, greatly surprised me. I expected to find a squalid Southern village. . . . What I found was a country town full of charm and even beauty—a somewhat smallish but nevertheless very attractive Westminster or Belair.

The houses are surrounded by pretty gardens, with cool green lawns and stately trees. The two chief streets are paved from curb to curb. The stores carry good stocks and have a metropolitan air, especially the drug, book, magazine, sporting goods and soda-water emporium of the estimable Robinson. A few of the town ancients still affect galluses and string ties, but the younger bucks are very nattily turned out. Scopes himself, even in his shirt sleeves, would fit into any college campus of America save that of Harvard alone.

John T. Scopes in Dayton with Dudley Field Malone (left) and Clarence Darrow (right). (UNITED PRESS INTERNATIONAL PHOTO)

It was his last mild column. After that, he had the time of his life. What he couldn't find, he made up—a mountaineer "expert" called Buckshot Morgan, a revivalist preacher, Elmer Chubb, who could survive poison snake bites and swallow potassium cyanide to prove he had faith. Justice or truth had little to do with the picture of the mountain culture, the "yobs" and the "yokels," that Mencken sent out day after day to the nation's newspapers. It was fun.

Mencken's first sight of "that yap schoolteacher" was when John Scopes nearly knocked him down with his now familiar little yellow car—so familiar that he had to be a dirt-track racer to get away from reporters. Scopes had just brought his father to the great meeting of the aging fighters that he had fomented. The Scopes family was so poor the father had to leave after three days. No one thought to invite him to stay on to see his son stand up in court in defense of everything he believed. By that time, the leading actors in the trial of the man whom Mencken called "the infidel Scopes" had taken over the whole stage.

John Scopes was still worried. He went swimming in Richland Creek every day and tried hard to remember something that was bothering him.

13

The First Day

By nine o'clock on the morning of Friday, July 10, 1925, it was as hot in Dayton as the place where the Fundamentalists wanted to send Clarence Darrow. The seven-hundred-seat courtroom still smelled of new paint and varnish. The judge's bench was freshly stained a bright cherry red. All the seats were filled. Three hundred people stood at the back of the room.

The crowd was made up mostly of men. Except for a few of the more emancipated, the women of eastern Tennessee stayed at home. The courtroom was a sea of clean white shirts with the high stiff collars worn by country men when they came into town, and suspenders. The snap-brimmed Stetsons of the farmers and the hard, shiny straw hats of the townsmen and city lawyers littered the benches or were clutched in laps. Paper fans, with pictures of Jesus, or mothers and children, or advertisements saying, "Do your gums bleed?" already moved back and forth. From time to time a man would bring out a huge handkerchief and mop his whole head, or flick away the flies drawn to the sweat.

Trials had always been a popular form of entertainment with the mountain people when they came into town. That is why mountain courtrooms were built so big. Some of the still-faced, rawboned, moustached men had parked their long shotguns against the wall, as northerners might park umbrellas. It made the "foreigners" nervous. The reporters sent out dispatches saying that the atmosphere was dangerous. They did not bother to find out that country men usually brought their guns on their long dirt-road treks into the county seat by buckboard so that they could shoot much-needed meat along the way. Who could have told H. L. Mencken, wiggling with delight at the sight of the "yokels," that game birds eat road pebbles and clean their wings in road dust?

At the table for the prosecution on the right of the judge sat General A. T. Stewart—the Attorney General—General Ben McKenzie, his son Gordon McKenzie, the Hicks brothers, Wallace Haggard, and William Jennings Bryan, Jr., who had come from Los Angeles to assist his father. In a rocking chair, wearing a collarless silk shirt with a handkerchief tucked in his neck, country-style, to catch his sweat, the master of the show, William Jennings Bryan, rocked back and forth and fanned himself with a big palm-leaf fan.

At the defense table, young Scopes, in a hand-painted bow tie new for the occasion, sat with Malone, Hays, Neal, and a friend of Darrow's who had dropped in for the first day of the trial. Darrow, sporting a pair of bright blue suspenders, sat rumpled and thoughtful in his seat. Everybody except Malone was in his shirt sleeves. Malone remained cool-looking in a double-breasted English suit. Palm-leaf and paper fans went on fluttering like butterflies all over the courtroom. Throughout the trial, Bryan moved his fan like a metronome. The courtroom had high windows on three sides; the sun and light

William Jennings Bryan and his son, William Jennings Bryan, Jr., at Dayton. (WIDE WORLD PHOTOS)

poured in. There was a hum of conversation, expectancy. From outside the windows, on the courthouse lawn, came the murmur of people gathered to listen to the trial on loudspeakers. Once in a while the "oogah" of a Ford horn was heard.

At nearly 9:30 A.M., Judge Raulston called the court to order. It was all a bit late because the judge, the prosecution, and the defense had had to pose for picture after picture for the world press. Judge Raulston, a typical Tennessee country judge, was trying to be affable to the visitors, reporters, and lawyers alike.

Finally he rapped his gavel. The trial was on.

"The Reverend Cartwright will please open court with prayer," the judge announced.

Brother Cartwright's voice went on and on. ". . . And to this end we pray that the power and the presence of the Holy Spirit may be with the jury and with the accused and with all the attorneys interested in this case." Murmurs of "amen" and "yes, yes" sounded throughout the courtroom. Darrow fumed. It all sounded like one of William Jennings Bryan's sly Fundamentalist tricks. The voice droned on, rose and dipped in the revivalist way from which both Bryan and Darrow had learned their style of speaking: ". . . that the affairs of church and state may be so administered that God may beget unto Himself the greatest degree of honor and glory. Amen." Darrow growled, but kept his peace for the time being. It was not yet time to attack. He was waiting for bigger game than a country preacher.

Much misunderstanding throughout the trial was caused by the outsiders' ignorance of and indifference to cultural habit. The same men who would have defended the study of anthropology and a respect for the customs of primitive people were blind to different cultural habits in their own country. They read the crowd as hostile, because of the guns and the amens and the peppering of honorary generals, colonels, and captains. Military titles have always been a form of politeness in the

mountains. They are a hangover from the pre-Revolutionary
War militia—the force that formed the basis of Washington's
Revolutionary Army. The British called them "rattlesnake colonels." They said that if a "provincial" killed one rattlesnake, he
became a colonel. If he killed two, he became a general. In
eastern Tennessee, what was once a slur had become a form of
courtesy. It was only later that the press and the powerful men
of the defense realized that many of the spectators had come to
listen and to learn.

Judge Raulston welcomed the foreigners, and the trial
began.

General McKenzie rose for the first business of the trial. "If
the court please, in this case we think it is proper that a new
indictment be returned." Neither side quite trusted the hurried
grand-jury decision that had been made in May so that the trial
could be set forward. A new grand jury was drawn and sworn
in. The same indictment as in May was read to them. Then the
judge picked up another book. His voice rose a little, as people's do when they read from the Good Book.

"In the beginning God created the heaven and the earth."

In the back someone whispered, "Amen."

"And the earth was without form, and void; and darkness
was upon the face of the deep. And the Spirit of God moved
upon the face of the waters."

He read to the grand jury, for the record, and to the court
the whole of the first chapter of Genesis.

The grand jury retired to hear evidence and consider its
verdict.

There was only one thing wrong. The witnesses that were
needed had run to the hills. They were the boys whom Scopes
had taught. He was their most popular teacher, and they did
not want to get him into any more trouble than he was in already.

John Scopes volunteered to find them. He knew they would

refuse to come out for anyone else. While the court adjourned and everybody stretched and walked out among the trees on the lawn, and T. T. Martin the revivalist sought to carry out his vow and harangued H. L. Mencken about his lost city soul, John Scopes rounded up the boys and convinced them it was all right to testify that he had taught evolution. Darrow saw that he needed to have a talk with the state's star witnesses if the trial was to go on.

Finally, at 11:00 A.M., the grand jury returned the new indictment and Judge Raulston spoke.

"Gentlemen and Mr. Attorney General, I am calling now for trial Case No. 5232, the State of Tennessee versus John Thomas Scopes."

Darrow interrupted the proceedings with the question that was to harass the court and the defense for the rest of the trial —the question of the admission of scientific witnesses.

At the beginning, both John Randolph Neal and William Jennings Bryan had, in essence, agreed on what the Scopes trial was about. Bryan had said, "It is the easiest case to explain I have ever found. While I am perfectly willing to go into the question of evolution, I am not sure that it is involved. *The right of the people, speaking through the legislature, to control the schools which they create and support is the real issue as I see it.*"

John Randolph Neal, in that short time when his cool mind controlled the planning of the defense, had in part said the same thing—but the emphasis of what he said was almost directly opposed to that of Bryan. "*The question is not whether evolution is true or untrue, but involves the freedom of teaching, or what is more important, the freedom of learning.*"

By the morning of July 10, all this had been almost forgotten. Out at the Mansion sat a battery of expert witnesses, called to Dayton to speak on the side of evolution.

Arthur Garfield Hays, who was sitting beside Darrow when

Clarence Darrow, standing in shirt sleeves at center, addresses the court on July 10, 1925. Behind him in shirt sleeves, seated and leaning forward with his arms folded, is John T. Scopes. Dudley Field Malone, in dark suit, stands at right. (CULVER PICTURES)

he got up to speak, said later that it was the beginning of "a battle between two types of mind—the rigid, orthodox, accepting, unyielding, narrow, conventional mind and the broad, liberal, critical, cynical, skeptical, and tolerant mind."

It would take eight days of trial to decide, not whether Scopes was innocent or guilty, not even whether evolution or the Bible was true, but falteringly and dimly to discover which side was the more rigid and unyielding.

"We have arranged for a considerable number of scientists who will—who are all busy men and we do not want to take them away from their work any longer than we need to, so I thought we ought to get an idea of just how soon we would need them after we start," Darrow said.

Raulston refused to be hurried. Deliberateness was to be his only defense against the giants in the incredible fight over which he had to preside and for which his few years of schooling at Fiery Gizzard, Tennessee, had left him utterly unprepared. All he had to fall back on was mountain slowness, and he used it. He suggested that even busy men could wait until the jury was chosen.

Chosen it was, and its selection took the rest of the first day of the trial. There were only sixteen men called to serve, from whom to choose the "twelve good men and true." When Darrow, who was used to being able to choose from hundreds for large city juries, objected to the narrowness of choice, he was told that for a misdemeanor it was not usual to call a regular panel, but that if he liked he would be allowed to choose anybody from the courtroom audience or the people on the courthouse lawn. Many a southern jury had been chosen from among the men lounging on the courthouse steps. Finally, out of deference to Darrow, the judge agreed to call extra men.

"Step up here, Colonel Darrow," Judge Raulston said.

He had given Darrow a title along with the prosecution, a sort of equality of politeness.

After a lunch recess, Judge Raulston got a little boy to

Courtroom scene at the Scopes trial. Members of the jury sit in the foreground. (PHOTO FROM THE BETTMANN ARCHIVE)

perch on the corner of the bench and draw the names of the jurors out of a hat. By 4:00 P.M., twelve had been chosen from the sixteen candidates and three additional men. They consisted of an ex-coal miner, eight farmers, two landowners, and a shipping clerk. Their religions were: six Baptists, three Methodists, one Southern Methodist, one Disciple of Christ, and one of no church. One of them was illiterate, three admitted to reading only the Bible. Most of them had the sunken cheeks, the jutting facial bone structure, and the flat, patient look of mountain men—watchful, untrusting, attendant.

John Scopes's father watched the jury file out and shook his head, worried. "Say, brother," he said, "that's a hell of a jury!"

That day, Dayton experienced the first traffic jam in its history. People cranked their stalled Fords and sweated in the punishing late-afternoon heat as the crowds gradually cleared for the weekend. Most of the visitors went to the cool mountain resorts, to Chattanooga, or to Knoxville. John Scopes went up on Walden's Ridge to the Saturday-night dance, to dance with the pretty girls in their newly bobbed hair and to forget about the ordeal that was becoming so painful to all his instincts for quietness and tolerance.

There, for the first time since he had been indicted, an incident happened that showed that an element of viciousness had crept into the proceedings. A high-school girl whom he had known for some time asked him to walk with her through the darkened area between the dance pavilion and the hotel because she was nervous of the dark. It seemed a reasonable request from a shy girl. As they reached the darkened part of the path, she suddenly threw her arms around his neck and kissed him passionately. He was paralyzed with surprise. As she held him, floodlights went on and he was caught in their crosslight. He heard cameras click. The next day, pictures of the sinner Scopes defiling the purity of one of his students were released to the press.

Down in the town it was fighting hot. As preachers and sinners gathered and argued and bootleg whiskey from the mountains had a roaring sale, fights broke out. Arguments about God ended in bloody noses. The five policemen had a hard time keeping the peace.

All day long on Sunday, preachers of every denomination held forth in the eleven churches, on the courthouse lawn, in the hot canvas tents.

Politeness was wearing thin as passions flared. In the Reverend Howard Gale Byrd's church, Charles Francis Potter of the West Side Unitarian Church in New York had been invited to preach. Potter had come down to testify for the defense on one of Darrow's main points—that a man could be a Christian, and an "eevolutionist" as well. The women of the congregation threatened to tear up the church if he was allowed to speak. In disgust, Byrd resigned his pulpit. He was the second person, after Scopes's sister, to lose his job owing to the passions of the Scopes trial.

It was T. T. Martin, the evangelist, who finally invited Potter to preach on Sunday evening. Outside the courthouse, against the wall and under the trees, a large platform of raw wood had been built for people who wished to hold meetings. Potter followed William Jennings Bryan, who gave one of his typical sermons about "evolutionary slime." Potter spoke gently and not for long, and not directly on evolution. Afterward, several young people came up to question him. He said later that they looked over their shoulders to be sure no one would notice them as they did it. One of them told him that they would probably be reported to their churches and publicly called down for speaking to him. "But I'm glad I heard you, sir," one of them added. "It was worth it. I aim to hear more of that kind of preaching when I get to be on my own."

Out at the Mansion, where the defense had its headquarters, the weekend was spent in a council of war. From the windows came a sound almost unknown locally; it was the sound of intellectual investigation being enjoyed by adults.

Rabbi Herman Rosenwasser of San Francisco was translating the Bible for the scientific witnesses. "Adam," he told them, meant "any living organism containing blood." He had set up a large chart with Hebrew characters. Rosenwasser either read or spoke Hungarian, Hebrew, Latin, Greek, French, and Italian. First he would translate the Hebrew characters into German, with a choice of several words in German for each Hebrew character, then in turning the German into English, he would show what a choice there was in the second translation. It was to point out that the Bible the Fundamentalists swore by was just such a translation, from Hebrew and Aramaic to Latin and then to English, that Rabbi Rosenwasser was waiting to take the stand. He was only one of the battery of expert witnesses whom Darrow had collected to help crush Bryan and, with him, what in Darrow's eyes was the stupidity that passes for innocence.

14 ✐

The Week of the Monkey

On Monday the trial began in earnest, in a series of false starts, delaying actions by both sides, and again almost sickening heat. While the fans waved and shirt collars wilted and people were treated for heat prostration, the prosecution and the defense moved slowly against each other. Much of the evidence was allowed only for the record. Raulston was careful to protect the jury from any facts that might prejudice them—any smack of evolutionary or scientific evidence.

The defense made a formal move to quash the indictment. Neal read part of the constitution of Tennessee. McKenzie spoke on the right of the legislature to control the teaching in the schools. General Stewart made a long definition of the duty of the legislature to "cherish literature and science." The fans went on waving and the voices droned on in the quiet, dulling tones of an ordinary country trial.

Then, in midafternoon, Clarence Darrow shambled up to speak to the court. New life ran through the hot, airless courtroom. He began softly. The spectators relaxed. There was nothing to fear in this man; he looked and talked like just the kind of country lawyer they were used to. Gradually his voice rose, preacher style, but with one of the most biting intelligences in the country behind it.

He quoted the Constitution. He quoted the Bible. He quoted Charles Darwin. After an hour of this, his voice rang out:

I will tell you what is going to happen, and I do not pretend to be a prophet, but I do not need to be a prophet to know. . . .

If today you can take a thing like evolution and make it a crime to teach it in the public school, tomorrow you can make it a crime to teach it in the private schools, and the next year you can make it a crime to teach it to the hustings or in the church. At the next session you may ban books and the newspapers. Soon you may set Catholic against Protestant and Protestant against Protestant, and try to foist your own religion upon the minds of men. If you can do one, you can do the other. Ignorance and fanaticism is ever busy and needs feeding. Always it is feeding and gloating for more. Today it is the public school teachers, tomorrow the private. The next day the preachers and the lecturers, the magazines, the books, the newspapers. After a while, your Honor, it is the setting of man against man and creed against creed, until with flying banners and beating drums we are marching backward to the glorious ages of the sixteenth century, when bigots lighted fagots to burn the men who dared to bring any intelligence and enlightenment and culture to the human mind.

Bryan went on rocking, fanning himself, and waiting. Since the beginning of the trial he had not said a word.

Clarence Darrow arguing his case during the Scopes trial. (KING FEATURES PHOTO)

On Tuesday morning, Darrow opened the argument by objecting to a prayer at the beginning of the day. He said it might prejudice the jury. His petition did more harm than good. He had stepped on a tradition in Judge Raulston's court, and it was like stepping on a sore toe. After the day before, Darrow was feeling carelessly triumphant. He did not even care very much when General Stewart called him "the agnostic counsel for the defense."

When the court convened on Wednesday afternoon, Malone made a statement for the defense. In it, if Bryan had only listened, were the first faint warnings of the attack the defenders of Scopes were preparing to make on him. Malone turned Bryan's own radical past on him as a weapon.

"We shall prove our philosophy and principles from the lips of witnesses who are a part of the prosecution," Malone said.

He went on:

The theory and opposition to the Tennessee anti-evolution law under which the defendant Scopes has been indicted cannot be more completely expressed than in the words of a great political leader who made the comment that I shall read, twenty years ago, on Thomas Jefferson's statute for establishing religious freedom. . . .

He said in the first place that to attempt to compel people to accept a religious doctrine by act of law was to make not Christians but hypocrites. That was one of the reasons, and it was a strong one. He said, too, that there was no earthly judge who was competent to sit in a case and try a man for his religious opinions, for the judgment of the court, he said, would not be a judgment but the personal opinion of the judge.

Malone went on to quote the "great political leader's" defense of freedom of speech, thought, and religion. Then he ended,

Those words were written by a member of the prosecution in this case, whom I have described as the evangelical spokesman of the prosecution, and we of the defense appeal from his Fundamentalist views of today to his philosophical views of yesterday, when he was a modernist, to our point of view.

The attack from his own youth seemed to flow off Bryan with less cause for annoyance than the flies and the sweat. When Stewart, of the prosecution, objected, Bryan waved him aside with his palm-leaf fan. He smiled at the judge and the spectators and spoke for the first time at the trial. "I require no protection from the court," he said. "At the proper time I shall be able to show that my position now differs not at all from my position in those days."

Then the witnesses for the prosecution were called to the stand. Three of them were the young boys whom Scopes had had to root out of hiding on the first day. Darrow had coached them all. They seemed to be extremely well grounded in the theories of evolution that Scopes had reviewed for examination on one of the few days when he substituted for the biology teacher. When Darrow cross-examined them, he spoke like a kindly uncle. To fourteen-year-old Howard Morgan, he reviewed the evolution theory and then asked:

"That's about what he [Scopes] taught you. It has not hurt you any, has it?"

"No, sir," Howard told the court.

After calling Walter White and F. E. Robinson to the stand to tell the story of what had happened in Robinson's drugstore and of the arrest of Scopes, but, of course, not the reasons for it, and after reading from the first two chapters of Genesis for the record, the state rested its case.

In midafternoon the first witness for the defense was called. It was Maynard M. Metcalf, of Johns Hopkins University, one

The jury in the Scopes trial waits outside the courthouse in Dayton while parts of the testimony are debated inside. (BROWN BROTHERS PHOTO)

of the country's leading zoologists. Darrow had to be content with questioning Metcalf "for the record" while the jury waited out on the lawn. He did not need to worry about their not hearing. Loudspeakers were wired in the branches of the trees. The sound of the trial voices hung over Dayton.

After a series of easy preliminary questions, Darrow asked, "Will you tell what it means, the fact of evolution?"

"Evolution, I think, means the change; in the final analysis I think it means the change of an organism from one character into a different character. . . ."

"Now in the classification of scientists, zoologists, where does man come?" Darrow asked.

"He is classed among the primates," Metcalf answered.

Man is not a very highly evolved animal in his body. He isn't as highly specialized as a great many organisms. His hand, for example, is a very generalized structure, nowhere near as much specialized as the hand of a bird, but he clearly belongs among the mammals. A group well up, I think, toward what we could call the well-elaborated members of that group physically.

There was a learned little titter from the scientists in the otherwise stunned courtroom.

The awed and silent crowd listened intently. This was not argument, nor passion. This was, for the first time in the trial, intelligent comment by a man who obviously knew what he was talking about. Respect for learning went deep with the people of the mountains. Most of them had only had a chance to slake their thirst for knowledge of the outside world on the words of circuit-riding preachers. Even Judge Raulston forgot which side he was on, and that he was running for office the next year, and leaned forward to listen.

At last, an actual lecture on evolution had been admitted to a Tennessee courtroom, even though it had to be done without the jury's being present.

After the day's proceedings, one boy was heard to say, "Don't you think Mr. Bryan is a little narrow-minded?"

When the mothers of the boys who testified that day were asked what they thought of the teaching of evolution after hearing Metcalf's testimony, Howard Morgan's mother said, "The teaching of evolution hasn't hurt me or my boy. I don't think any of us here in the mountains have studied evolution enough. I wish I knew more about it."

Harry Shelton's mother laughed when she was asked. She said, "As far as I'm concerned, they can teach my boy evolution every day of the year. I can see no harm in it whatsoever. Why, when they called Bud to testify against Mr. Scopes, he had forgotten most of his lessons. He had to get the book out and study it up."

15 ✍

Combat by Speeches

The fifth day of the trial opened, as most of the others had, with the knotty problem of whether scientific testimony should be admitted as evidence. Darrow stormed. He opened the proceedings with a statement long prepared, in which, without quite realizing it, he confessed why he had come to Dayton.

> We expect to show by men of science and learning—both scientists and real scholars of the Bible—men who know what they are talking about . . . first, what evolution is, and, secondly, that any interpretation of the Bible that intelligent men could possibly make is not in conflict with any story of creation, while the Bible, in many ways, is in conflict with every known science, and there isn't a human being on earth believes it literally.

No one seemed to understand that in his way Darrow was trying to use a courtroom as naïvely as William Jennings Bryan. Bryan was trying to prove divine revelation in a court

The impact of the Scopes trial was felt all over the nation. Judge, a magazine of humor, published an Evolution Number with a cover featuring William Jennings Bryan. (CULVER PICTURES)

of law, and Darrow was trying to make a court of law pass on the validity of a scientific theory. Neither was to succeed.

Judge Raulston has been castigated since, and he was at the time, for refusing to admit the expert evidence on evolution. There is some reason to give him credit for the fact that he was trying to keep the case within the confines of the original indictment. *Did John Scopes break the law of Tennessee by teaching a theory contrary to the Butler Act?* What that theory was, decided Raulston, was not the court's business. As the days passed, the argument over expert scientific testimony was becoming an obsession with Darrow.

Finally, on Thursday afternoon, Bryan was ready to speak. Although they had heard him on the courthouse lawn on Sunday, this was the speech the people. had been waiting for. When word got out, the lawn was crowded with people, gathered around the loudspeakers, sitting on the grass, leaning against the hoods of cars. The courtroom was so crowded that Judge Raulston asked the spectators to be very quiet. He was afraid the floor would collapse under the strain of a demonstration.

Bryan began gently, easily, almost fumblingly, in the best tradition of American cracker-barrel oratory and preaching. It was a classic technique of persuasion used by Will Rogers, by Billy Sunday. It was easy to listen to. It made everybody feel comfortable and secure. Then the great silver voice began to rise against the foreigners, the outsiders, the educated. Bryan spoke deridingly of the "gentleman from New York" and got a laugh. He spoke tenderly of the little children. Then he hit one of the high points of the speech he had been writing for the six weeks since he had decided to come to Dayton.

Tell me that the parents of this day have not any right to declare that children are not to be taught this doctrine? Shall not be taken down from the high plane upon which

God put man? Shall be detached from the throne of God and be compelled to link their ancestors with the jungle; tell that to these children? Why, my friends, if they believe it, they go back to scoff at the religion of their parents! And the parents have a right to say that no teacher paid by their money shall rob their children of faith in God and send them back to their homes, skeptical, infidels, or agnostics, or atheists!

He played on their mountain shyness before the educated, the old refrain of the politicians since the mountain men could vote:

I suppose this distinguished scholar who came here shamed them all by his number of degrees. . . . I can understand how my friends felt when he unrolled degree after degree. Did he tell you where life began? Did he tell you that back of all these that there was a God? Not a word about it. Did he tell you how life began? . . . They do not dare to tell you that it began with God and . . . ended with God. They come here with this bunch of stuff that they call evolution, that they tell you that everybody believes in . . . and they do not explain the great riddle of the universe—they do not deal with the problems of life—they do not teach the great science of how to live—and yet they would undermine the faith of these little children in that God who stands back of everything and whose promise we have that we shall live with Him forever by and by. They shut God out of the world.

He was deep into the sermon he had been giving all across the country since he took up the Fundamentalist cause. He spoke of the Virgin Birth, the Resurrection, the Atonement. He reminded his listeners of all the Fundamentals that he and they were protecting in the hot courtroom. People began to moan and call out "amen," "yes, yes," as they were used to doing at such sermons. No one stopped Bryan. The court had refused all scientific evidence, but Judge Raulston did not stop a pure Fundamentalist sermon from being preached in his court. . . . He was up for office the next year.

The beautiful voice of William Jennings Bryan ebbed and flowed, played and sang over the courtroom, out through the loudspeakers, thundered up and down the Tennessee Valley. He ended quietly.

> The facts are simple, the case is plain, and if those gentlemen want to enter upon a larger field of educational work on the subject of evolution, let us get through with this case and then convene a mock court, for it will deserve the title of mock court if its purpose is to banish from the hearts of the people the Word of God as revealed!

There was a great wave of applause. Bryan sat down and fanned himself and smiled. It was the hour he had been waiting for.

Then Dudley Field Malone got up slowly and took off his coat. The erudite, civilized Catholic from New York began to answer Bryan—not Bryan the revivalist preacher or Bryan the politician, but Bryan the secretary of state for whom Malone had once worked and whom he had respected. Nobody expected much from the man Bryan had called derisively "the gentleman from New York."

Malone, too, began quietly.

> If the court please, it does seem to me that we have gone far afield in this discussion. . . .

> I have been puzzled and interested at one and the same time at the psychology of the prosecution, and I find it hard

"HE LOVES ME, HE LOVES ME NOT!"

In summer, 1925, cartoonists all over the country found a ripe subject in the Scopes trial and William Jennings Bryan. (CULVER PICTURES)

to distinguish between Mr. Bryan, the lawyer in this case, Mr. Bryan, the propagandist outside of this case, and Mr. Bryan, who made a speech against science and for religion just now, and Mr. Bryan, my old chief and friend. . . . He is not the only one who believes in God; he is not the only one who believes in the Bible.

Malone went on:

There is a difference between theological and scientific men. Theology deals with something that's established and revealed. It seeks to gather material which they claim should not be changed. It is the word of God, and that cannot be changed. . . . The scientists say, take the Bible as a guide, as an inspiration, as a set of philosophies and preachments in the world of theology.

A new thing was happening in the court. Passion was at last being linked with intelligence. Malone was as deeply involved in his beliefs as Bryan and Darrow, but he had not let his mind atrophy into irrevocable dogma—or, in the case of Darrow, irrevocable doubt. The spectators began to hang on his words as they had on no one else's.

And we say, "Keep your Bible. Keep it as your consolation, keep it as your guide. But keep it where it belongs, in the world of your own conscience, in the world of your individual judgment, in the world of the Protestant conscience that I heard so much about when I was a boy. Keep your Bible in the world of theology, where it belongs, and do not try to tell an intelligent world and the intelligence of this country that these books, written by men who knew none of the accepted fundamental facts of science, can be put into a course of science. . . ."

Malone answered Bryan's accusation about the perversion of children's minds, and his answer brought, not "amens," but a sigh of sanity and approval in the hot, packed room.

We have no fears about the young people of America. . . . If any teacher teaches the boys or girls today an incredible theory, we need not worry about those children of this generation paying much attention to it. The children of this generation are pretty wise. . . . The least that this generation can do, your Honor, is to give the next generation all the facts, all the available data, all the theories, all the information that learning, that study, that observation has produced; give it to the children in the hope to heaven that they will make a better world of this than we have been able to make of it.

Malone, too, had waited a long time to say what he had to say that afternoon, to defend knowledge against credulity, and the open human mind against those who close and stultify it in any name, religion or otherwise. His voice followed Bryan's out over the loudspeakers and into the valley, into the dead silence of thousands of entranced people.

We are ready to tell the truth as we understand it. And we do not fear all the truth that they can present as facts. We are ready. We are ready. We feel we stand with progress. We feel we stand with science. We feel we stand with intelligence. We feel we stand with fundamental freedom in America. We are not afraid. Where is the fear? We meet it! Where is the fear? We defy it!

Malone's speech was over. There was a moment of silence, and then, like a storm, the cheering began.

Scopes later told what the effect on Bryan was:

I have never seen such a great change hit a human being as fast as it did Bryan. Malone spoke for not more than twenty minutes. There was only dejection on Bryan's face; the victory that had been his only a few moments before was suddenly, disastrously dissipated.

The courtroom had gone wild. No one heeded the warning about the strain on the floor. No one heard the gavel. It was as if a hungry people had suddenly been fed. One of the police pounded so hard with his billy club that he broke a table. "I'm not pounding for order," he shouted. "I'm cheering!"

Clarence Darrow was heard to mutter some of the saddest words in the whole trial: "Tennessee needs only fifteen minutes of free speech to become civilized."

When the courtroom cleared, only Scopes, Malone, and Bryan were left. Bryan had not moved from his rocking chair. He let his palm-leaf fan drop to the floor and stared at it. Without turning his head, he said to Malone, "Dudley, that was the greatest speech I have ever heard."

"Thank you, Mr. Bryan," Malone said gently. "I am sorry it was I who had to make it."

16

The End of a Career

On Friday, Judge Raulston opened court by ruling that expert scientific testimony was irrelevant to the case. Darrow fought all day against the decision. He was sixty-eight years old, and he had been running up against the same brick wall all week—the refusal of Judge Raulston to allow the scientific evidence on which he had based his defense. At last he lost his temper.

"We want to make statements here of what we expect to prove," he shouted at Raulston. "I do not understand why every request of the state and every suggestion of the prosecution should meet with an endless amount of time, and a bare suggestion of anything that is perfectly competent on our part should be immediately overruled."

Raulston bristled, "I hope you do not mean to reflect upon the court?"

"Well, your Honor has the right to hope," Darrow replied.

All weekend, people wondered if Darrow would be cited for contempt of court. Many of the reporters were no longer interested. With Malone's speech and the sight of Bryan wilting under it, they felt that the most exciting part of the trial was over. Besides, it was too hot to breathe in Dayton. Not for one day or night of the trial had the heat abated. Even the few thunderstorms had not shifted it.

By Sunday, many of the spectators, the sideshows, the tame chimpanzees, and the religious lunatic fringe had left Dayton. Not so, Darrow and Bryan. Neither had gained the chance he had come for. Bryan had somehow to retrieve his reputation after Malone's searing speech. Darrow had had a list of fifty-five questions in mind ever since he wrote the public letter that Bryan had refused to answer.

Both of them were old, hidebound men, but neither of them knew it. Bryan at sixty-five and Darrow at sixty-eight had come down roads of training that made them represent, like two cliffs across a gulf, the two sides of the schism that had split the nineteenth century.

All weekend, Bryan worked on the speech that was to retrieve what he had lost under fire from Malone. It was to be, he said, "the mountain peak of my life's effort."

Whatever Darrow was planning he was keeping to himself and the other defense lawyers. There was little, after all, that he could do. His whole defense had been thrown out of court. He could not call the witnesses he had brought to Dayton from all over the country. His outburst on Friday probably meant that he would be jailed or fined for contempt of court. But even with all the forces against the defense, there was laughter at the Mansion on Sunday night.

Hays had thought of a brilliant plan. When he and Darrow explained it to Dr. Kirtley F. Mather, one of the unheard expert witnesses, he offered to help them rehearse. Mather was a Baptist, and a geologist from Harvard University. For hours the two lawyers fired questions at him while he played a part. They had a hilarious time.

In the meantime, Bryan was speaking his Sunday sermon

Clarence Darrow and William Jennings Bryan pose for a photograph in Dayton, Tennessee. Bryan clutches his ever-present palm-leaf fan. (WIDE WORLD PHOTOS)

across Walden's Ridge. Something had crept into it that would be heard tingeing the language of the mountains for a long time. It was one thing for the young to go away to the cities and come back embittered by being made fun of for their ways. It was another for the city to come to them.

The city was H. L. Mencken. They knew everything that he had said about them. The *Chattanooga News* had published it all. Such an offense against hospitality shocked, hurt, and angered them. Bryan had no qualms about rubbing it in, again and again, until the mountain people who heard him were raw with bitterness. Bryan's voice was as strong as ever, but only five hundred people had gathered to listen to him. If it was an omen, he did not seem to see it.

17

Under the Water Oaks

Clarence Darrow thought that the earth's crust must be thin under the Bible Belt and that the heat came from the hell underneath. Dayton had wilted. In the courtroom the flies buzzed over the sweat that poured from the people crowding the room to the walls. They had come this time to see Judge Raulston give the agnostic outsider, Darrow, his comeuppance. When the judge entered the courtroom he looked grim. He said that the court and the state of Tennessee had been treated without courtesy. He cited Darrow for contempt and set his bond at five thousand dollars. After more argument on the central question of scientific evidence, Judge Raulston finally allowed brief summaries of the expert testimony to be read into the record, but without the jury being present. Once more the members of the jury were asked to leave the courtroom. They had observed less of the trial than any of the spectators. Again they went out and sat around the courthouse lawn under the loudspeakers.

While Judge Raulston had barred expert testimony as evidence, he had no objection to its being read into the record.

From the questions he asked from time to time, he seemed to be fascinated.

All morning, Hays read statements of the defense while the crowds from all over the surrounding country increased outside. Strange words were dropping from the outside microphones while Hays read résumés of the expert testimony for the court record. The crowds heard that men had been on the American continent for an estimated ten thousand years, that life had existed on earth for "not less than fifty million years," that the oldest fossils of humans that had been found up to 1925 went back only twenty-five thousand years. Then, the crowds heard the words of Dr. Maynard Metcalf, who on the Wednesday before had told them the first facts about the evolutionary theory.

> God is just as truly and just as intimately acting in the gradual growth of a plant from a seed or of a man from a fertilized egg as He would be in creating the full-grown plant or man all at once in a thousandth part of a second of time.

> There is no conflict, no least degree of conflict, between the Bible and the fact of evolution, but the literalist interpretation of the words of the Bible is not only puerile—it is insulting, both to God and to human intelligence.

> But the fundamentalist would do much worse than insult God. He is, in reality, although he doesn't realize this, trying to shut men's minds to God's ever-growing revelation of Himself to the human soul.

At just before noon, the court was adjourned for lunch.

By half-past one, when the court reconvened, the largest crowd of the whole trial had gathered. There seemed little reason for it. There was only the voice of Hays, monotonously reading into the record the evidence of a whole new world of revelation—nothing exciting enough for many of the nation's leading reporters to bother to cover. They had filed many millions of words on the summer madness at Dayton. Nothing more could happen to titillate or amuse. The world news media were a little bit tired of Dayton.

Minute by minute, by some kind of unspoken telepathy, the crowd grew and spilled over the two acres of courthouse lawn.

When Darrow returned after the lunch recess, he seemed a contrite man. He apologized to the court, to the judge, and even to the state of Tennessee. Darrow was after bigger game than a country judge, and he had to persuade the judge to withdraw the charge of contempt so that he could speak.

Judge Raulston forgave him, not only in the name of the court, but in the name of the state. He quoted poetry. He quoted the Bible. It was the only real chance Judge Raulston had to make a speech and he took it. At the end, the two men shook hands and the crowd in the courtroom applauded.

By two o'clock the heat in the courtroom was appalling. The building was old, and the crowd large. "I am afraid of the building," Judge Raulston said. He ordered the court down onto the courthouse lawn where the platform had been built for outdoor speeches. It was the stage from which Bryan had preached for the two previous Sundays. The courtroom spectators streamed down the wide stairs and swelled the throng of two thousand people outside.

Chairs, tables, and spittoons were brought down and put onto the platform. Little boys shinnied up the great trees that shaded it, and gazed down from the branches. Bryan, instead of his rocking chair, found himself a nice country-lawyer chair, where he could rear back and swivel around. His palm-leaf fan moved slowly back and forth. The huge gathering that stretched out over the lawn, on car tops, out of windows, on the wooden sawhorse benches that the revivalists used at night, were his own people. He was as comfortable as in his living room and he looked it. He knew he had to, or the people would lose faith in him. Once more he sat before them, the great William Jennings Bryan, risen from perpetual, challenging defeat. Under the trees it was more comfortable. There were even a few cloud flecks, bringing hope of rain.

The court settled down to the drone of Hays's voice reading the scientific evidence into the record softly so that the jury, sitting fifty feet away, directly under a loudspeaker, could not hear him. Darrow saw red when he noticed a huge sign saying READ YOUR BIBLE, painted on a board, just in front of the jury. He demanded that it be removed. All in all, it seemed an ordinary afternoon. Hays introduced a Hebrew Bible and a Catholic Bible into the record. Then, just as quietly, in midafternoon, Hays rose to ask the bench a question.

Malone whispered to John Scopes, "Hell is going to pop now!"

Hays said, "The defense desires to call Mr. Bryan as a witness."

Bryan's fan froze in his hand. Judge Raulston held his breath. No one moved. Then there was a great sigh among the crowd.

All the attorneys for the prosecution sprang to their feet at once and began to shout objections. Bryan jumped to his feet and insisted that Darrow, Malone, and Hays should also then be called.

"Call anybody you desire. Ask them any questions you wish," said Judge Raulston.

The court, the prosecution, the crowd went silent as Bryan walked toward Darrow. Firmly and calmly he said, "Where do you want me to sit?"

To witnesses he seemed cheerful, self-confident, even a little cocky. After all, he had studied the Bible for years. No one in the country knew it better. Hardly anyone had spoken more words in its defense. Not the Hebrew Bible, or the Catholic

Bible, or the King James Version, but the BIBLE. He was ready for anything Darrow might do.

Judge Raulston gave him a last chance to back out of the trap Darrow had been setting for him ever since the publication of the fifty-five questions. Darrow was still waiting to ask them—every one of them.

"Mr. Bryan, you are not objecting to going on the stand?" Judge Raulston called.

"Not at all," said Bryan. He seated himself, smiled politely at Darrow and the crowd, and began to fan himself again. His head, in profile, looked noble. Before him, the rumpled, wrinkled Darrow looked like an old bulldog.

They began politely, both complete professionals, both trained in the nineteenth-century political style. Even the props were for the crowd—the palm-leaf fan, the blue suspenders, Bryan's comfortable lounging in front of Darrow—as if Darrow were asking a favor of him—Darrow's homely, rumpled old underdog pants.

"You have given considerable study to the Bible, haven't you, Mr, Bryan?" Darrow began. His voice was friendly, even disarming.

Bryan said he had studied the Bible for about fifty years.

"Do you claim that everything in the Bible should be literally interpreted?" Darrow had come to Dayton to ask that question.

Bryan had come to answer it. He even hoped to ride into the United States Senate at the next election on his answer. A note of lecturing crept into his voice. "I believe everything in the Bible should be accepted as it is given there." He saw a chance to make Darrow look foolish and he took it. "Some of the Bible is given illustratively. For instance: 'Ye are the salt of the earth.' I would not insist that man was actually salt, or that he had flesh of salt"—Bryan smiled and his crowd smiled back. They were just below him, pressed close to the platform, close enough to reach down and shake hands with.

Darrow smoothed his sparse hair and thought a bit. His voice was still quiet. He questioned almost as if he wanted to learn. "But when you read that Jonah swallowed the whale"— from the crowd came a slight titter—"or that the whale swallowed Jonah—excuse me please—how do you literally interpret that?"

Carefully and quickly Darrow had maneuvered Bryan into absurdity and Bryan seemed not to know it yet. They argued about whether it was a whale or a big fish, or whether it was made for the purpose.

"You believe that the big fish was made to swallow Jonah?" Darrow sounded incredulous. He had tipped the balance a shade too far and Bryan became wary.

"I am not prepared to say that; the Bible merely says it was done."

"You don't know whether it was the ordinary run of fish, or made for that purpose?"

"You may guess. You evolutionists guess," Bryan snapped.

"But when we do guess, we have a sense to guess right," Darrow snapped back.

Darrow was driving home point after point to trap Bryan into sounding inane. He was trying to control his long-pent-up anger.

Did Joshua make the sun stand still? Did the sun at that time go around the earth? Did the man who wrote the Book of Joshua think the day could be lengthened or the sun could be stopped?

Bryan's voice rose lamely out of the barrage of questions, "I believe he was inspired."

Did the sun stand still or did the earth? Bryan conceded it might have been the earth.

"Now, Mr. Bryan," Darrow went on, "have you ever pondered what would have happened to the earth if it had stood still?"

"No."

"You have not?"

"No; the God I believe in could have taken care of that, Mr. Darrow."

"I see. Have you ever pondered what would naturally happen to the earth if it stood still suddenly?"

"No."

Darrow's voice rose to a crescendo, in the best oratorical style. "Don't you know it would have been converted into a molten mass of matter?"

There was a roar from the crowd as from a single mouth; not laughter, but something else.

The two men were forgetting the crowd. Both their voices had risen. Bryan gripped the arms of his swivel chair. Darrow leaned over him, his shirt soaked in sweat, and asked question after question.

The questions and answers snapped back and forth faster and faster. Bryan was getting as flustered as Darrow wanted him to. Bryan was passionately defending his religious beliefs. Darrow was blindly attacking the bigotry he had fought all his life.

"You believe the story of the Flood to be a literal interpretation?"

"Yes, sir."

"When was that Flood?"

Bryan did not know.

An airplane flew over the courthouse and everybody, including the judge, looked up. Airplanes were still a novelty.

"I would not attempt to fix the date. The date is fixed . . ."

There was discussion of an estimated date based on the Bible.

"What do *you* think?" asked Darrow.

"I do not think about things I don't think about," Bryan grumbled.

"Do you think about things you *do* think about?"

"Well, sometimes."

Laughter raked over the courthouse lawn.

Gradually Darrow was slipping beyond the pale of argument for evolution, for freedom of thought, or teaching, or discovery, or doubt. Never had his theory that man is the blind product of his heredity and his environment been better acted out than on that afternoon in the shade of the maple trees and the water oaks in Dayton, Tennessee. Darrow was no longer a sixty-eight-year-old successful lawyer, urbane, civilized, questioning, intelligent. He could no longer see Bryan, the man. He saw only the old stupidity, the cruelty, the arrogance. He was a small-town boy trying to deride, ridicule, and destroy the blind bigotry that had stunted his beloved father's life.

Later, Darrow wrote, "I was truly sorry for Mr. Bryan. But I consoled myself by thinking of the years through which he had busied himself tormenting intelligent professors with impudent questions about their faith, and seeking to arouse the ignoramuses and bigots to drive them out of their positions. It is a terrible transgression to intimidate and awe teachers with fear of want."

Stripped away from Bryan were all his protections of fame and brilliance, his fantastic talent as an orator, and the love of his followers. He sat before intelligence, the one attribute he had ignored, belittled, and hidden from since he, the unquestioning son of a small-town Puritan father, had succeeded as Americans succeed, through being popular—like the heroes of Horatio Alger and a thousand matinees—as a defender of the right, his country, and his God.

It was a slaughter.

He was asked about other cultures, the ancient past, Buddhism, Confucianism, religious origins. Bryan knew nothing of them.

"Did you ever investigate them?" Darrow went on relentlessly. The questions kept on. "Have you ever tried to find out?" "Did you ever read a book on primitive man?" "Have you read any?" "Where have you lived all your life?"

After an hour and a half, Bryan hardly knew what he was saying. He sounded almost witless. His face was dark, suffused with blood, and his hands were trembling. Then Darrow sprang the final trap.

He asked quickly and quietly, "Do you think the earth was made in six days?"

"Not six days of twenty-four hours," Bryan answered.

The Fundamentalists gasped. Bryan, their champion, had denied the literal interpretation of the Creation!

Darrow had the crowd with him now. He entertained them. It was hard to hear Bryan. Something had happened to the famous silver voice.

The prosecution tried to stop the questioning, but Judge Raulston refused. Anyway, neither of the old men could be stopped.

"The purpose," yelled Bryan, "is to cast ridicule on everybody who believes in the Bible, and I am perfectly willing that the world shall know that these gentlemen have no other purpose than ridiculing every Christian who believes in the Bible."

"We have the purpose," Darrow shouted, "of preventing bigots and ignoramuses from controlling the education of the United States and you know it, and that is all."

Malone tried to interfere. "Mr. Bryan seems anxious to get some evidence into the record . . ."

There was no hope of quieting or protecting Bryan. "I am not trying to get anything into the record. I am simply trying to protect the word of God against the greatest atheist or agnostic in the United States," he shouted over Malone's voice. There was prolonged applause from the crowd.

Finally, in his own fury at the scene in front of him, Malone insisted on speaking. "Your Honor . . . I would like to say that I would have asked Mr. Bryan—and I consider myself as good a Christian as he is—every question that Mr. Darrow has asked him for the purpose of bringing out whether or not there is to be taken in this court only a literal interpretation of the Bible or whether, obviously, as these questions indicate, if a general and literal construction cannot be put upon the parts of the Bible which have been covered by Mr. Darrow's questions. I hope for the last time no further attempt will be made by counsel on the other side of the case, or Mr. Bryan, to say the defense is concerned at all with Mr. Darrow's particular religious views or lack of religious views. We are here as lawyers with the same right to our views. I have the same right to mine as a Christian as Mr. Bryan has to his, and we do not intend to have this case charged by Mr. Darrow's agnosticism or Mr. Bryan's brand of Christianity."

There was a great burst of applause from the courthouse lawn. But it did not stop the two old men. Once more they began to wrangle. They had degenerated into mutual inanities —Darrow a triumphant clown, Bryan floundering in defeat.

Darrow picked up the Bible and began to read: " 'And the Lord God said unto the serpent, Because thou hast done this, thou art cursed above all cattle, and above every beast of the field; upon thy belly shalt thou go and dust shalt thou eat all the days of thy life.' Do you think that is why the serpent is compelled to crawl upon its belly?"

"I believe that."

"Have you any idea how the snake went before that time?"

"No, sir."

"Do you know whether he walked on his tail or not?"

"No, sir, I have no way to know."

There was a howl of laughter from the crowd.

Suddenly Bryan's voice rose, screaming, hysterical: "The only purpose Mr. Darrow has is to slur at the Bible. . . . I want the world to know that this man, who does not believe in a God, is trying to use a court in Tennessee—"

"I object to your statement." Darrow was contemptuous. "I am examining you on your fool ideas that no intelligent Christian on earth believes."

Judge Raulston put an end to the argument by adjourning the court.

That night, at last, it rained.

Most of the remaining reporters were jubilant about the day's events. They had enjoyed the fight. Some of the southern ones struck the note of unthinking bitterness that is an instinctive, almost animal, reaction when southern heroes or protective beliefs are questioned.

With less bias than the others, and with a greater sense of history, Paul Y. Anderson sent a dispatch to his newspaper in St. Louis:

A memorable scene was enacted yesterday afternoon beneath the great maples that canopy the yard of the Rhea County courthouse. On a platform, where was convened the trial of John T. Scopes, Clarence Darrow placed William Jennings Bryan on the witness stand, and what followed was an event in the intellectual history of the world. It was magnificent and tragic, stirring and pathetic, and above all it was pervaded by the atmosphere of grandeur which befitted the death grapple between two great ideas.

Two old men, one eloquent, magnetic and passionate, the other cold, impassive and philosophical, met as the champions of these ideas and as remorselessly as the jaws of a rock crusher upon the crumbling mass of limestone, one of these old men caught and ground the other between his massive erudition and his ruthless logic. Let there be no doubt about that. Bryan was broken, if ever a man was broken. Darrow never spared him. It was masterly, but it was pitiful.

It was profoundly moving. To see this wonderful man, for

after all, he was wonderful, this man whose silver voice and majestic mien had stirred millions, to see him humbled and humiliated before the vast crowd which had come to adore him was sheer tragedy, nothing less.

It had been, for so many years, both the genius and the instinctive reaction of Bryan to fight back. Stripped, with his profound ignorance—unbelievable in a public man whose reputation was built on what he said—exposed as with a scalpel, he still planned a rebuttal. Then Stewart, the attorney general, had to break the news to him that he would not get a chance to put Darrow on the stand and question him in turn. Stewart felt it was his duty to bring the trial back within the limits he had fought for all the time. The point was not whether God in six days created the world or whether man was evolved out of eons of change from the protozoa, but whether John T. Scopes committed a misdemeanor by breaking a Tennessee state law.

The men quarreled half the night. The next morning an almost silent Bryan let the trial end. His testimony was stricken from the record. The jury found John Thomas Scopes guilty as charged and Judge Raulston fined him a hundred dollars. The Scopes Monkey Trial was over.

John Scopes was still worried. He had finally remembered what had been worrying him all through the trial. He found one of the reporters he had made friends with and asked him to go for a drive.

"I've got something on my mind," he said.

For a while they drove around the shaded streets of Dayton. The crowds had already thinned out and the town was quieting down almost to normal.

Scopes parked his little car outside of town on a country road. The silence deepened as he shut off the engine.

"There's something I must tell you. It's worried me," he said. "I never taught that evolution lesson. I skipped it. . . . I'm convicted of a crime I never committed."

John T. Scopes stands before the judge as he is sentenced in Dayton. (BROWN BROTHERS PHOTO)

18

The Death of Bryan

Bryan's defeat was not yet over. For the next few days the two angry old men threw questions and answers back and forth at each other. Each, entrenched in the remainder of his life, went on biting at the other. Bryan forgot a thing he had never forgotten before—his dignity. He questioned Darrow by the same method he had scorned two years before—the newspapers. Darrow, the obvious victor, answered intelligently, magnanimously. He could afford to. By an accident of birth and training he, at sixty-eight, happened to land on the side of the future and to serve it well. Bryan's and the country's tragedy was that his talents could only serve the past. In so many ways, the two men were as alike as brothers—brilliant, persuasive, nineteenth-century reformers, believing naïvely that anything could be decided in a court of law by a jury of twelve good men and true, if only they could be persuaded, seduced, cajoled, and, as a last resort, informed.

By Sunday, the twenty-sixth, Bryan felt better. He had tried out before two audiences the new, the final, speech that was going to show the world where he stood on God, democracy, and the Bible. The audiences, the people whom the agnostic evolutionists had called "yokels," loved it.

Bryan ate one of the enormous Sunday dinners he was used to and went upstairs in the rented Dayton cottage where the greatest fight had been waged, the fight with himself in the face of shattering public defeat. He lay down to take a little nap. When his servant went to call him, he found that Bryan had died in his sleep.

His death, better than the last days of his life, served the Fundamentalist cause. He became a martyr. But even martyrdom cannot bolster a fading crusade. In the first flush of what they tried to claim as a victory, the Fundamentalists only succeeded in getting one more law passed. That was in Mississippi. Later, in 1927, an antievolution bill passed in Arkansas. That was the end.

The country had passed its Fundamentalist phase. The frightened people who backed it found, as always, new shadows to fight, new scapegoats. Where once those of questing intelligence were accused of being "agnostic," "atheistical," or "eevolutionist," the shadows took on new shapes, and the new words of accusation became "communist," "egghead," and even the once-mild "liberal." Instead of backcountry fears of intelligence being played on by Bryan, as they had been until his defeat at Dayton, by the fifties a far more sinister use was being made of the protective dogmas of fear in the investigations of Senator Joseph McCarthy.

The fight had the same impetus—the freezing fear of change. For democracy, unlike any other modern form of government, uses the ability to change, to bend without breaking, as one of its great strong sources of energy. It is the one form of government that thrives on questions. There will always be those who fear this quality, who will yearn to flee to the safety of dogma, for the war between the security of blind acceptance and the insecurity of intelligent questioning is international and is never-ending.

19 ✑

Aftermath

The Scopes case was appealed, but it never got beyond the Tennessee courts. The country was tired of it, and the state of Tennessee embarrassed. The Tennessee supreme court reversed Judge Raulston's decision on a technicality, and killed the case.

Fortunately, John Scopes was not entirely forgotten by the thinkers he had represented at his trial. While the expert witnesses waited at the Mansion to testify, they made up a scholarship fund that was enough to put him through two years of graduate geology study at the University of Chicago.

The world he had served was not quite through with him. In the spring of 1927, he applied to a well-known technical school for a fellowship. The president of the school administering the fellowship endowment told him to "take his atheist marbles and go elsewhere."

Scopes died in 1970. He had never taken advantage of the vast light of publicity that had been turned on him when he was so young, nor had he let it defeat him. Quietly he served for forty years as a geologist, some of the time in South America, far away from ballyhoo, fame, and notoriety.

It took until this generation for an antievolution law to be overturned. The first "anti-monkey" law to be stricken down by the United States Supreme Court was that of Arkansas. In 1965, Susan Epperson, a twenty-four-year-old biology teacher at Central High School, in Little Rock, brought a case to test, once again, the constitutionality of antievolution laws and their effect on the freedom of teaching.

In 1968, her case reached the Supreme Court at last, and a decision was handed down. The law was declared unconstitutional because it established a religious doctrine, and this violated both the First and Fourteenth amendments to the Constitution. The decision made hardly a stir in a country that had long since forgotten the great Monkey Trial.

In 1970, Mississippi's law against the teaching of evolution —the last such state law in the nation—was overturned and declared unconstitutional by the state supreme court.

"The decisions of the Supreme Court of the United States which interpret the Constitution of the United States are binding upon us and we have no choice other than to follow such decisions," the Mississippi court said.

Finally, after forty-five years, the fight begun at Dayton had been won. It was to strike down and declare unconstitutional a law designed to limit the freedom of teachers to, in Malone's words on a hot afternoon back in 1925, "give the next generation all the facts . . . in the hope to heaven that they will make a better world of this than we have been able to make of it."

Selected Bibliography

Darrow, Clarence. *The Story of My Life*. New York: Charles Scribner's Sons, 1932, 1960.

DeCamp, L. Sprague. *The Great Monkey Trial*. New York: Doubleday & Company, Inc., 1968.

Ginger, Ray. *Six Days or Forever? Tennessee v. John Thomas Scopes*. Boston: Beacon Press, 1958. (Paperback, Chicago: Quadrangle Books, Inc.)

Grebstein, Sheldon Norman. *Monkey Trial: The State of Tennessee vs. John Thomas Scopes*. Boston: Houghton Mifflin Company, 1960.

Scopes, John T. and Presley, James. *Center of the Storm: Memoirs of John T. Scopes*. New York: Holt, Rinehart and Winston, 1967.

Index

About the author

A native of Charleston, West Virginia, Mary Lee Settle teaches at Bard College, Annandale-on-Hudson, New York, for one term a year. For the remainder of the year she writes—either novels or history. She was twice awarded Guggenheim fellowships for her work on *The Beulah Trilogy*. Her interest in the Scopes trial sprang from research into the historic causes of anti-intellectual prejudice in the South, for the *Trilogy*, and also from one of her earliest memories— of being teased by her brother's chanting, "Your old man's a monkey." Her latest novel, *The Clam Shell*, was published in January, 1972. She is at present working on a study of the lasting democratic and puritan effects of the English revolution of the seventeenth century.